# SIKHISM
## AND
## GURU GRANTH SAHIB

**AUTHOR OF**
1. Strange But True in Sikhism
2. Guru Tegh Bahadur
3. Guru Granth Sahib——A Critical Study
4. Outlines of Sikh Thought
5. Philosophy of Guru Nanak
6. Travels of Guru Nanak
7. Sikh Ethics
8. The Sword And The Spirit
9. The Life And Ideals of Guru Gobind Singh
10. A Conceptual Dictionary of The Adi Granth
11. The Sikh and The Khalsa

# SIKHISM
## AND
# GURU GRANTH SAHIB

## Dr. Surindar Singh Kohli

NATIONAL BOOK SHOP
Pleasure Garden Market,
Chandni Chowk, Delhi-110006

Rs. 150

**SIKHISM AND GURU GRANTH SAHIB**
Dr. Surindar Singh Kohli

*Published by :*
**NATIONAL BOOK SHOP**
Pleasure Garden Market,
Chandni Chowk, Delhi-110006
Phone : 011 - 23278392
e-mail : nbs_books@sify.com

Ist Edition - 19 90
ISBN 81-7116-093-X

N.B. Shop, Delhi Reprint- **2007**
ISBN 81-7116-394-7

*Printer :*
**B. K. OFFSET**
Delhi-110032

# CONTENTS

**BY THE SAME AUTHOR**

The Ninth Nanak, History of Punjabi Literature, Guru Grath Sahib : An Analytical Study, Dictionary of Guru Granth Sahib, Dictionary of Mythological References in Guru Granth Sahib, The Sikh Philosophy, Yoga of the Sikhs, The Sikh Prayers, Sikhism and Major World Religions, Outlines of Sikh Thought, Sikh Ethics, Life and Ideals of Guru Gobind Singh (based on original sources), Sikh Predictions, Philosophy of Guru Nanak, Travels of Guru Nanak, A Conceptual Encyclopaedia of Guru Granth Sahib, The Sikh and Sikhism, Death and After, Naam and Real Sikhism.

# PART I

# SIKHISM

# Foreword

This small book on Sikhism is an attempt to give an over-all picture of Sikhism in a nutshell. A Sikh has been defined in the light of Sikh scriptures. The misunderstanding regarding the origin of Sikhism has been discussed and clarified. The salient features of Sikhism have ben discussed so that the reader gets an idea about its Philosophy and Religion. The successors of Guru Nanak Dev never swerved from the path preached by the Founder; hence there is constant unity of Sikh Thought. The Sikh Religion and culture have contributed a great deal towards human uplift. *The Adi Granth* (Guru Granth Sahib) is the main scripture of the Sikhs. It embraces all the humanity and presents a universal religion. The Sikh history is the history of trials and tribulations. The Sikh Martyrs stand unparalleled in the history of the world. All the constituents of Sikh society have equal status. The woman has a significant position in Sikhism.

The fundamentals of Sikhism are given hereunder:

1. God is One without a second.
2. All the so-called gods and goddesses are His Creation and prone to death.
3. Therefore God alone is to be worshipped.
4. We must seek the help of the Guru (spiritual preceptor) for realisation of God.
5. All human beings are equal in the eyes of God.
6. The woman is not at all inferior to man.
7. The soul is a part and parcel of God and can attain Unity with Him.
8. In order to be one with God, godly qualities are to be imbibed.
9. An ideal person *(Gurmukh)* is an amalgam of action, devotion and knowledge.
10. To keep up one's spiritual progress, *Sadh Sangat* or the company

1

of good people is necessary.

11. The path of householders is the best. The objective is not attained through renunciation.

12. Work is worship, therefore one should work for the welfare of the family and society.

13. As far as possible one should help the needy. Service, social service or public service helps one in his spiritual progress.

14. The individual must attend to his duties regarding the three planes viz. physical, moral and spiritual. Without imbibing virtues (qualities), one cannot rise on the spiritual plane.

15. The remedy of all the ills is the remembrance of the Name of the Lord, for which one must seek the guidance of the Guru.

16. That food is to be avoided, which makes one insane.

17. The education should make one sane and serviteur of society.

18. The well-being of the whole world should be the motto of a Sikh.

I am confident that this small volume will prove valuable asset for the Sikh world and will be received warmly by the students and scholars of Sikhism throughout the whole world.

Surindar Singh Kohli

# The Definition of a Sikh

The word "Sikh" has been derived from the Sanskrit word "Shishya", which according to the Sanskrit-English lexicon means 'A pupil; disciple; scholar'. A person admitted to an educational institution may be called a *Sikh* or *Shishya*. Every profession has a training institute which under the guidance of a mature teacher or Guru, imparts training to a *Shishya* in that profession. In this article, the word *Sikh* connotes that pupil or disciple, who gets training regarding godly qualities in the school of the True Guru, known as *Sat Sangat* (The True Congregation):

> "*Sat Sangat* (The True Congregation) is the school of the True Guru, where (The Sikh) gets training in godly qualities" (Var Kanra M.4, p.1316).

The True Guru is the teacher, who gives instruction regarding the Lord and makes the Sikh (student) wise:

> "O my Lord, we are Your ignorant children. Blessed is the Guru-teacher (The True Guru), who has made us wise by giving us instructions regarding the Lord" (Gauri Bairagan M.4, p.168).

The Guru is the spiritual teacher, who destroys the darkness of ignorance. In order to differentiate such a Guru from the ordinary teacher, sometimes the word "Satguru" (The True Guru) has been used and also in order to differentiate the Sikh of the True Guru from an ordinary pupil, the word *Gursikh* has been used in the *Adi Granth* and the Vars of Bhai Gurdas.

Except the first (or the Primal) Guru, all the other Gurus were primarily *Gursikhs*. Bhai Gurdas may be quoted in this connection:

3

The Lord Himself Created the True Guru Nanak Dev.
Guru Angad, the Gursikh came to Baba (Nanak Dev).
Guru Amar Das is Gursikh, who was liked by True Guru.
Ramdas was Gursikh and was called the Guru.
Guru Arjan, the Gursikh, became the Guru.
Hargovind, the Gursikh, could not be concealed.

(Var 20, Pauri 1).

These verses make it clear that after the first Guru, all the Gurus from Guru Angad Dev to Guru Hargobind were all Gursikh in the beginning and then became the Gurus. After Guru Gobind Singh, the Guruship was bestowed on *Granth Sahib* (the *Adi Granth*) for all times. Therefore after the Tenth Master, any great Gursikh, may become Guru-like, but cannot become a Guru. Because of the observance of the discipline of the Guru *en toto,* a Gursikh may become one with the Guru. Guru Ram Das says:

> There remains no difference between the Guru and the Sikh because of the observance and instruction of the same discipline of the Guru (Asa M.4, p.444).

Bhai Gurdas also writes in the same strain:

> A Spiritual Wonder became manifest when the personality of the Sikh merged in that of the Guru (Var 20, Pauri 3).

But to become Guru-like, the Sikh has to pass through a very difficult process. It is like winning the game of chess. Bhai Gurdas says:

> The Sikh of the Guru, after listening to the instructions of the Guru, was called a Sikh. The Sikh listened attentively the instructions of the Guru. After listening, the Gursikh, accepted everything in his mind with reverence. This Gursikh was liked and loved by other Gursikhs. The Gursikh went into the company of other Gursikhs. The Gursikh won this difficult game of chess played with thirty-two pieces. (Var 20, Pauri 19).

The Gursikh, having been instructed by Gurudeva practises it with a firm

4

mind and preaches the discipline to other seekers. The Gursikh meets a Gursikh. They all gather in a holy congregation and hold talks about their spiritual development. The Guru is an ocean, filled with gems and pearls and the Sikhs are like swans, who trade in such treasure. Guru Arjan Dev says:

> The True Guru is the ocean of pearls, one attains it according to his Writ. The Sikhs like swans gather together according to the Will of the True Guru. The ocean is full of gems and pearls, the swans eat them, but the ocean always remains full. The Lord Wills that the ocean and the swans are not separated. Only that Sikh comes to the Guru, on whose forehead this Writ is recorded from the very beginning. Such a Gursikh not only ferries across the world-ocean himself, but also saves his family and the whole world. (Var Ramkali M.5, p.960).

The practical life of a *Gursikh* makes him swim across the ocean of *Samsara* along with many others. He can even get the release of the whole world. Then the question arises: what are those gems and pearls which the *Gursikh* pecks from the Guru-ocean and becomes so powerful, that the Tenth Master calls him as "Mera Sikh" (My Sikh). The Guru says, "He who remains within discipline, is my Sikh". It becomes clear from this quotation that the *Gursikh* has a significant and definite discipline, which should be discussed here. The life of a *Gursikh* is in tune with the discipline of the Guru. The instruction of the Guru is full of gems, rubies and pearls. Guru Nanak Dev says in *Japuji:*

> "If we listen to the instruction of the Guru, our intellect becomes full of gems, rubies and pearls".

The same thought has been expressed by Guru Ram Das in the following manner:

> "O my Gursikh friend, follow the Path of the Guru. Whatever the Guru says, act upon it faithfully; the story of the Lord is queer" (Dhanasari M.4).

## The Discipline Followed by a Gursikh:

(a) The Guru performs two functions in relation to a Gursikh. He gives the WORD or NAME to the Sikh and also Knowledge. The Word of the Guru is called *Naad* and the knowledge *Ved*. Both of them are present in the *bani* of the Guru. Therefore it is the primary duty of a *Gursikh* that he should search the gems and pearls in the *bani* (compositions) of the Guru. This *bani* is also Guru because the spirit of the Guru is present in this *bani*. The ambrosia and nectar lie hidden in this *bani:*

> *Bani* is the Guru and Guru is the *Bani*, all the ambrosia is within this *Bani*. Whatever is written in *Bani*, the devotee should act upon it reverently, the Guru will, assuredly, grant him release. (Nat M.4).

The *Bani* of the Guru is a great benefaction for humanity. Those who are saturated with this *Bani*, they only are Gursikhs:

> "Nanak utters the nectar-like *bani*, which is liked and loved by Gursikhs; The Perfect and True Guru gives instructions through this *bani*, which is his act of philanthropy (Majh M.4).

(b) Guru Ram Das has expressed the way of living of a *Gursikh* in the following manner:

> "He who calls himself a Sikh of the True Guru, he should get up in the early hours of the morning and remember the Name of the Lord. He should make effort to rise before the day dawns and take a bath in the pool of nectar. Under the instructions of the Guru, he should repeat the *mantram* of the Guru, all his troubles will end and all his sins and blemishes will be destroyed. Then when the day dawns, he should sing the *bani* of the Guru and remember the Name of the Lord while sitting or moving. He who remembers my Lord with every breath and loaf, that *Gursikh* is liked by the Guru. He on whom my Lord showers His Blessings,

6

the Guru instructs that *Gursikh*. I beg for the dust of the feet of that *Gursikh* who not only repeats the Name of the Lord but also makes others to repeat it." (Var Gauri M.4).

The following facts come before us from the above hymn:

1. The *Gursikh* rises up early in the morning and takes a bath.
2. Then he remembers the Name of the Lord.
3. When the day dawns, he sings the *bani* of the Guru.
4. Throughout the remaining day, either working or sitting or moving, he repeats the Name of the Lord with every breath. This shows that he is always in tune with the Lord.
5. He, not only, remembers the Name of the Lord himself, but also makes others remember the Lord.

He remains firm on this instruction in *Japuji:* "One should remember the Name of the Lord at the ambrosial hours in the morning and utter and participate in the Praises of the Lord".

(c) The *Gursikh* wages a war and conquers the five mighty vices i.e. lust, anger, greed, attachment and ego. He is a wrestler of the Lord and has within himself the strength of the Word of the Guru. Guru Arjan Dev says:

> "I am the wrestler of the Lord; I feel highly elated on meeting the Guru. All the participants have gathered and the Lord Himself is Seeing all this. The musical instruments and trumpets are being played; the wrestlers are taking rounds and I have defeated the five youths on having been blessed by the Guru. All have gathered together; they will return home with changed routes. The *Gurmukhs* (Enlightened Ones) will go benefitted and the *Manmukhs* (self-willed) will even lose their principal. (Sri Rag M.5).

Only the *Gurmukh* or *Gursikh* will win in this tough contest and the *Manmukh* will suffer defeat.

7

(d) *Gursikh* is blessed with the Grace of the Lord. The Name cannot be remembered without His Grace. The Lord Himself gives prominence to His devotees in His *Hukam* (Will) and with His Power makes all others subservient to *Gursikhs*. But this Grace is only achieved on taking steps forward on the True Path enunciated by the Guru. Guru Ram Das says:

"To whomsoever the Lord Blesses Himself, He brings the whole world to his feet. One may feel afraid, if something is done by him, only the Lord Himself extends His Powers everywhere. Look, O brother, this Play of the True Lord, before Whose Might everyone has bowed. The Lord Protects His devotees and the faces of the calumniators and tyrants are blackened. The eminence of the True Guru always rises higher, who ever makes the devotees sing the Praises of the Lord. O *Gursikhs*, always remember the Name of the Lord, the True Guru and the Lord will make the life comfortable in your home. O *Gursikhs*, consider the *bani* of the Guru as True, the Lord Himself issues it through his mouth. The dear Lord Himself purifies the mouths of the *Gursikhs* and Himself makes the whole world proclaim loudly the Praises of the Guru. I am the servant of the Lord, Who Protects the honour of his servants (Var Gauri M.4).

(e) The *Gursikh* surrenders himself completely to the Will of the Lord. That is the reason why the True Guru is kind towards him:

The *Gursikhs* accept the Will of the Lord, therefore they are ferried across by the Perfect Guru. (Shalok Varan te Vadhik M.4).

(f) When the instructions of the Guru awaken in the heart of the *Gursikh*, he forsakes the unsteady intellect. All the darkness of his ignorance vanishes in the light of the knowledge of the Guru:

"When the instruction of the Guru awakens within, the unsteady intellect is forsaken. With the light of the instruction of the Guru, all the darkness disappears (Sorath M.1, p.599).

(g)   Even if the *Gursikh* may falter in his speech, he is always true to the
      Will of the Lord:

> "Even if they falter in speech, they are always True to the Will
> of the Lord" (Asa M.4).

Contrary to this, those who have sweet speech, but are full of poison
in their hearts, they remain separated from the Lord and are always
in agony:

> "Those who eat and wear without devotion towards the Guru,
> they may be considered as dead or born as cripples. Though they
> speak sweetly, they throw out poison from their mouths. They
> have wicked minds, therefore they are separated by the Lord"
> (Var Gauri M.4).

(h)   The *Gursikh* always leads a life of virtue and *Dharma*. According
      to Guru Ram Das such *Gursikhs* are not only pure themselves, but
      all the things coming in their contact are also pure:

> "Those who are absorbed in the Name of the Lord, all their
> eatables, clothes and maya are pure; their houses, temples,
> palaces and rest-houses are all pure, in which the *Gurmukhs*,
> devotees, and the praying Sikhs live or stay; their horses, saddles
> and sacks are all pure on which the *Gurmukh* Sikhs and saints
> take a ride; their actions of piety are all pure, who repeat and
> remember the Name of the Lord; those who are destined to be
> virtuous, such *Gurmukh* Sikhs go to the Guru" (Var Sorath
> M.4).

The True Guru is the field of righteousness and from him, the
Gursikh learns the Way of Dharma:

> "The True Guru is the field of Dharma, in which one reaps
> whatever one sows. The *Gursikhs* sow the nectar and get the
> ambrosial fruit of Hari. They are pure in both worlds and in the

9

Court of the Lord, they receive a robe of honour". (Var Gauri M. 4).

The *Gursikhs* sow nectar and reap nectar. They are honoured in both the worlds.

(i) The life of a *Gursikh* is saturated with godly qualities. He listens to and sings the Praises of the Lord depicting godly qualities:

> We have sung about the attributes of the Lord under all circumstances, having been befriended by the True Guru; just as the neem tree near the sandalwood tree takes the qualities of the sandalwood (Nat M.4).

By imbibing the qualities, the state of devotion is created. Guru Nanak Dev has written in *Japuji:*

> "There can be no devotion without the qualities".

God is Fearless, therefore the Gursikh becomes fearless:

> "Those who have remembered the Fearless Lord, all their fear is destroyed"
> (Asa M.4).

God is without enmity, therefore the *Gursikh* is without enmity:

> "None is my enemy and I am enemy of none" . . .
> "I have befriended all"
> (Dhanasari M.5, p.671).

God is Pure, therefore the *Gursikh* is also pure:

> "The Guru destroys the dirt of vicious intellect of the Sikh"
> (Gauri Sukhmani M.5). etc.

(j) The Perfect Gursikh is *Brahm Giani* (the Knower of Brahman),

10

whose attributes have been mentioned in Sukhmani like this:

*Brahm Giani* is always unattached like lotus in water. He is without any blemish like the quality of the sun drying everything. He sees everything alike like the quality of air for everybody. He has the quality of forbearance like the earth whether it is dug up or pasted with sandalwood. He has the quality of the spontaneity of fire. He is pure like the water. His mind is illumined like the earth from the sky. The friends and the enemies are alike for him. He is without pride. He is the highest, but still he considers himself lowest in his mind. Whomsoever the Lord Wills, he can become a *Brahm Giani*. *Brahm Giani* considers himself the dust of the feet of all. He has tasted the spiritual ambrosia. He is kind towards all. He bears no ill-will for anybody. He sees everything and everybody alike. The ambrosia trickles down from his eyes. He is free from any bondage and is absorbed in pure discipline. The knowledge is his food and he concentrates only on Brahman. He depends only on the One Lord. He is immortal. He is extremely humble and a spring of philanthropy. He always remains detached and has bound down the mercurial mind. Only good comes out of him and he always prospers. He ferries across everyone and all the world worships him.

All the above-mentioned attributes of a *Brahm Giani* are, in fact, the attributes of a *Gursikh*.

(k) The following characteristics of a *Gursikh* are mentioned in the Vars of Bhai Gurdas:

1. There are lakhs of superior, middling and inferior people, but the *Gurmukh (Gursikh)* considers himself the lowliest. He becomes the dust of the feet of others and loses his ego. He remains in the company of the saints and in the fear and Love of the Lord. He serves others like a servant.
   He is humble, serves others and speaks sweetly. He is absorbed in the Word and is honoured in the Court of the Lord. He

considers himself ignorant and is conscious of his short stay in the world. He detaches himself from all worldly hopes. Such a *Gurmukh (Gursikh)* attains the desired fruit and knows the Unknowable. (Var 8, Pauri 29).

2. I am a sacrifice to those Gursikhs, who get up in the early hours of the morning, who take a bath in the pool at the ambrosial hour, who remember the Guru with full concentration, who join the holy congregation and always sing and listen to the *bani* of the Guru, who remain in tune with the discipline, who, in devotion of love, celebrate the festivals in memory of the Guru and who remaining in service of the Guru, prosper. (Var 12, Pauri 2).

3. I am a sacrifice to him, who being powerful considers himself powerless, who being honourable considers himself humble, who being wise, considers himself ignorant, who surrenders himself before the Will of the Lord, who is attracted towards the Path of a *Gurmukh*, who being conscious of his short stay in the world considers himself only a guest—such a person is honoured both in this world and the next. (Var 12, Pauri 3).

4. I am a sacrifice to him, who follows the discipline of the Guru and remains humble in his heart, who does not go near the wife of another person, who does not touch the wealth of others, who does not listen to the calumny of others, who practises the instructions of the Guru, who sleeps and eats less-such a *Gurmukh* is absorbed in the state of *Sahaj* (the Supreme state). (Var 12, Pauri 4).

5. I am a sacrifice to him, who considers the Guru and the Lord as One, who fosakes duality, who does not think ill of even evil persons, who does not talk ill of any one, who deliberately suffers defeat, who performs acts of philanthropy and takes pleasure in them. In the carefree Court of the Lord, his modesty is rewarded. He recognises the Perfect Guru and the Word of the Guru (Var 12, Pauri 5).

6. I am a sacrifice to those *Gursikhs*, who lose their ego on meeting the Guru, who remain detached while living in *maya*, who are absorbed in the discipline and the Feet of the Guru, who meet other *Gursikhs* and convey the instructions of the Guru to them, who still their outgoing mind, who remain detached in the world

of hopes and who remain firm on the instructions of the Guru. (Var 12, Pauri 6).

(l)  In Raga Suhi of the *Adi Granth*, there are two hymns entitled *Kuchajji* and *Suchajji* by Guru Nanak Dev and one hymn entitled *Gunwanti* by Guru Arjan Dev. The life of a *Manmukh* has been depicted in *Kuchajji* (meaning without any decorum), but in *Suchajji* (a lady knowing decorum) and *Gunwanti* (a virtuous lady), we peep into the life of a *Gurmukh* or *Gursikh*. *Suchajji* surrenders to the Will of the Lord at every hour and every step and Gunwanti remains indebted to that *Gursikh*, who unites her with the Guru. Guru Arjan Dev says:

"If you forsake the advice of your mind and forget duality, you will have the Sight of the Lord and no trouble will come to you. I cannot speak on my own, whatever I have said, it has been uttered under the Will of the Lord. Guru Nanak Dev has extended his domain and bestowed on me the treasure of the devotion of the Lord. The thirst and hunger trouble me no more and I am fully satisfied. Any *Gursikh*, whom I see, I repeatedly bow at his feet."

Guru Nanak Dev has described the way of living of a *Gurmukh* (*Gursikh*) in this manner in *Siddh Goshta:*

A "Gurmukh" performs triple function of Nam (he remembers the Name of the Lord), *Dan* (he gives in charity to the deserving and needy) and *isnan* (takes physical and mental bath). He remains concentrated in *Sahaj* (the supreme spiritual state). He receives honour in the Court of the Lord. He is eminent and remover of fear. He remains under the discipline of the Guru and makes others follow this discipline. He unites others with the Lord. He has the knowledge of all religious texts (Shastras, Smritis and Vedas). He knows the secret of every heart. He is without enmity and rises above all worldly accounts. He remains saturated with the Name of the Lord and realises Him. The cycle of his births and deaths have ended and he receives honours in

13

the Court of the Lord. He recognises the good and the bad. He attains the state of *Sahaj*. He is absorbed in the Praises of the Lord's Court and is free from any bondage. He receives the Name of the Transcendent Lord and with the Word, he burns away the ego. He sings the Praises of the True Lord and remains merged in Him. With the True Name he receives high honours and gets knowledge of the whole world. He concentrates on the True Word and the True *bani* manifests through him. Rare are the persons who know the ecstatic state of his mind. He abides in his own spiritual home. He is a Yogi, who knows the method of Yoga and knows none else except the Lord. He conquers the mind by destroying the ego and is always absorbed in Truth. He conquers the world by defeating and driving away *Yama*. He never faces defeat in the Court of the Lord. He knows the Lord and unites others with Him. He recognises the WORD.

*(Siddh Goshta)*

(m) The *Gursikh* is a householder. He works and from his earnings, satisfying the needs of his family, he tries to fulfil the needs of the needy and afflicted ones. Guru Nanak Dev says about this *Gursikh:*

"He works and earns for his family and gives something in charity. He, thus, recognises the PATH' (Var Sarang M.4, Shalok M.1, p.1245).

Bhai Gurdas also says that such *Gursikhs*, living in maya, remain detached:

Ending their cycle of births and deaths, the philanthropists have come into the world. They instruct for the devotion of love and abide in the true region of holy congregation. They are like swans living in *Mansarovar* and are absorbed in the Word. They abide like sandalwood in vegetation and give fragrance to all, bearing or not bearing fruit. They are like the ships in the ocean of *Samsara* and ferry their families across it. They are uninfluenced by various waves and remain detached in maya. They are rewarded with the fruit of bliss and are absorbed in *Sahaj* (the

Supreme spiritual state)—(Var 12, Pauri 18).

(n) Keeping in view the above facts, the chief characteristics of a Gursikh are as follows:

1  A Gursikh is a householder.

2  He is a worker and from his earnings, he not only satisfies the needs of his family, but also helps the needy and deserving.

3  He practises the discipline of the Guru. He remembers the Name of the Lord and makes others remember it.

4  He joins the holy congregation and studies the bani of the Guru. He gives full respect to his brethren of the Faith.

5  He listens to the Praises of the godly attributes through *Katha* (discourse) and *Kirtan* (music) and also joins in the singing of the divine music.

6  He imbibes all the virtues including the godly qualities.

7  He loves everybody. He is fearless, without enmity and pure.

8  He is always ready to serve other beings. He sees in them the Light of the Lord.

9  He is always humble. Having been blessed with all the qualities, he considers himself the lowliest.

10  He does not touch the body and wealth of others. He rises above calumny.

11  He does everything under the Will of the Lord.

12  He is always in tune with the Lord.

13  He gets up in the early hours of the morning and regularly observes the discipline.

14  He eats less and sleeps less.

15  He conquers his mind and attains the Grace of the Guru and the Unity with the Lord.

16  He is a *sant* (saint), *Sadh* (hermit), *Gurmukh* (Enlightened one), *Brahm Giani* (Knower of Brahman) and *Jivan-Mukta* (Emancipated while living).

17  He receives robes of honour in both the worlds.

18  Having realised the Fourth State of *Sahaj*, he becomes a man of equal perception and a philanthropist.

(o) But the Path on which the *Gursikh* traverses, is very fine and it is very difficult to travel on it. It is sharper than the double-edged sword and finer than hair. Nothing equals this Sikhism in the past, present or future. The duality is destroyed in it and all matters of strife end. One finds solace only in the Love of the Lord. Bhai Gurdas says:

> *Gursikhi* is very fine and is like the taste of an insipid stone. It is sharp like the double-edged sword and finer than the hair. Nothing equals it in all the three tenses. The duality ends in it and one attains Unity. The second, third and all else is forgotten. All other attachments are destroyed and one get pleasure in one desire only. (Var 9, Pauri 2).

(p) The love of the *Gursikh* for the Guru is identical with the love of the child for the mother. Just as the mother brings up the child with every breath, similarly the True Guru makes the Sikh traverse on the True Path. Guru Ram Das says in this connection:

> The mother loves and the son eats; the fish loves to bathe in water; the True Guru loves to put his WORD in the mouth of a *Gursikh*. (Gauri M.).

Similarly:

> "The love of the *Gursikh* is to meet the Guru neck by neck"
> "The love of the *Gursikh* is to meet the Guru and be satisfied."
> "The love of the *Gursikh* is to come face to face with the Guru."
> (Gauri Guareri M.4).

(q) Several forms of a Gursikh are depicted figuratively in the *Adi Granth*:

1 They are the moneylenders and fortunate, who gather the Commodity of the Name of the Lord. One gets truth and purity from these saints. (Gauri Bawan Akhri M.5).

2 They are the wealthy and great traders, the True Guru has made

16

me realise it. (Maru Solhe M.1).

3   They are Blissful in all the four ages, who have the unending and infinite treasure of the Name (Sri Rag M. 3)

4   They are the friends and blissful saints, who are liked by their Lord (Vadhans M.5).

5   They are good (saints) and liked by You, on whom You have Bestowed the honourable place (Asa M.4).

6   They are Beautiful, who sit in the holy congregation; they have gathered the wealth of the Name. (Majh M.5).

7   They have become devotees, on whom You have bestowed Your Grace (Gauri Majh M.5).

8   Those who have concentrated on One Lord in the early hours of the morning, they are the Perfect kings, who have fully utilised their time. (Var Majh M.1).

9   They are the wise and clever beings who have remembered their Lord (Var Sorath M.4).

10  They are the real kings who have realised the Perfect Lord. They are carefree and remain in the only state of Love (Var Majh M.1, Shalok M.2).

11  They are the Bhagats (devotees) who are liked by You. I am a sacrifice to them (Malar M.5).

12  They are emancipated who conquer their minds and the *maya* has no impact on them . . . (Gujri M.3).

13  They remained protected, who met the True Guru. (Var Maru M.5).

14  They are blissful and in *Sahaj*, and having priceless qualities, they have come to save the world . . . (Vadhans M.5).

15  They are blissful and always Beautiful, who have destroyed their ego. (Var Malar M.1).

16  They are cool, who have realised the True Guru (Gauri M.5).

(r)  *Gurmat* (Sikhism) being a part and parcel of Bhakti Movement, *Gursikh* is a *Bhagat* (devotee). He has no belief in either *Karma Kanda* or *Upasana Kanda*. He worship only *Nirguna* (Transcendental) Brahman. He does not worship any form of *Saguna* Brahman. He has no faith in the incarnations, gods and goddesses. His Bhakti is *Antarang* or *Anuraga* Bhakti. It is also called *Bhae* Bhakti or *Prema* Bhakti i.e. devotion with love. In this devotion, there is no place for dancing. Guru Nanak Dev says:

> "Let intellect be the Musical instrument and love the drum and the mind be in the ecstatic mood. This is the real Bhakti and the ascetic practice; dance only in this pose with your feet (Asa M.1, p.350).

Since the *Gursikh* adopts the True Path, he is a saint, Since his face is turned towards the Guru, he is a *Gurmukh;* since he is a knower of Brahman, he is a *Brahm-Giani;* since he has attained release while living, by following the True Path, he is a *Jivan-Mukta.* He is a trader of the One Lord. He is the real serviteur of the Lord.

(s) Gursikh is a practising student of the school, of the True Guru. Abiding in the holy congregation, he gradually ascends the steps of the spiritual ladder. *Gursikhi* (Sikhism) is a journey, where an ordinary individual, practising the discipline of the Guru, steps forward and with the grace of the Guru, he ultimately reaches the final destination. Taking birth in *Dharam Khand* (the region of piety) and passing through *Gian Khand* (the region of knowledge), *Saram Khand* (the region of effort) and *Karam Khand* (the region of Grace), he reaches *Sach Khand* (the region of Truth). The mature *Gursikhs* and the Guru give him necessary directives. The present Guru is *Guru Granth Sahib.* The Guru is not a physical personality, it is the Word of the Guru. For this reason it is said that the form of the Guru is *Sabda.* Therefore it is the duty of a *Gursikh* to enter the spiritual sphere taking the support of *Guru-bani,* whenever he feels an obstacle, he should consult a mature Gursikh. Gursikhi (The Path of a Gursikh) is not a doctrine, it is a practice; its foundation is Dharma. Whereas a Buddhist takes the refuge in *Dharma, Sangha* and *Buddha,* the Gursikh takes the refuge in *Dharma, Sangat* (holy congregation) and *Brahman.* His song should be:

> "I have raised a *dharamsala* of Truth
> I have searched and brought together the *Gursikhs;*

18

I wash their feet and fan them and repeatedly bow at their feet.
(Sri Rag M.5).

(t)    Bhai Gurdas describes the importance of the human birth and the way of life of a *Gursikh* in the following manner:

"Out of the eighty-four lakh species, the important birth is that of a human being. He has been given the eyes to see, the ears to hear and the mouth to speak sweet words of love. He has been given hands to work and feet to move and go to the holy congregation. H has to work in the spirit of Dharma; he has to earn and to give in charity (to the needy). The birth of a *Gurmukh* is fruitful; he studies the *bani* of the Guru and listens to it with understanding. He satisfies the brethren of his faith and purifies his mouth with the nectar of the washings of their feet. He does not forsake the tradition of the Iron age *(Kaliyuga)* of bowing down at their feet. He himself swims across the ocean of *samsara* and makes other *Gursikhs* swim it. (Var 1, Pauri 3).

# The Origin of Sikhism

## I

Four religions originated in Indian sub-continent viz. Hinduism, Jainism, Buddhism and Sikhism. Hinduism is the oldest of the world-religions and Sikhism the youngest. Hinduism began in hoary antiquity, but Sikhism is a little older than five centuries. The name 'Hindu' has a geographical significance. It is a derivative from 'Sindhu', a name which was given to the area watered by Indus. Writing about the origin and nature of Hinduism Dr. T.M.P. Mahadevan writes: "The word 'Hindu' is only a corrupt form of 'Sindhu'. Hinduism meant the faith of the people of the Indus-land. This significance was lost even in the distant past. Not only did Hinduism become the religion of the whole of India, but it spread far and wide and became the faith of the colonies of Greater India, like Java, Malaya and Borneo. The indigenous names by which Hinduism is known are *Sanatana Dharma* and *Vaidika Dharma. Sanatana Dharma* means eternal religion and is expressive of the truth that religion as such knows no age. It is coeval with life. It is the food of the spirit in man. The other name *Vaidikaa Dharma,* means the religion of the Vedas. The Vedas are the foundational scriptures of the Hindus. Hinduism regards as its authority the religious experience of the ancient sages of India. It does not owe its origin to any historical personage or prophet. Buddhism, Christianity and Islam are founded religions. Their dates are definite, since their authors are known. No such date or founder can be cited as marking the beginning of Hinduism. Hence it is called *Sanatana* and *Vaidika*, ancient and revealed."[1]

Because of various internal upsurges and external invasions and approaches throughout the past centuries, Hinduism has been growing enormously. "Within its fold now there is room for numerous sects, such as Vaishanavas, the Shaktas, the Shaivas, the Sauras, the Ganapatyas etc.

20

Within each of these sects again there is room for numerous distinct groups. Moreover, the faith of the Jains, the Buddhas, the Sikhs, the Arya Samaj, the Brahmo Samaj also are derived from Hinduism".[2] Jainism, Buddhism and Sikhism are considered off-shoots of Hinduism. Buddhism and Jainism "separated from the parent religion early and maintained an independent existence, more or less, throughout their course".[3] Similarly Sikhism has also maintained an independent existence.

Hinduism is also called neo-Brahmanism. It is a synthesis of Vedic and non-Vedic. The Jainas claim antiquity for their religion because they believe in twenty-four Tirthankaras, the last of whom was Vardhamana Mahavira, the contemporary of Lord Buddha, the founder of Buddhism. Gautama Buddha was born in the sixth century B.C. Guru Nanak Dev, the founder of Sikhism was born in the fifteenth century A.D. (A.D. 1469). He had nine successors, the last of whom was Guru Gobind Singh, who passed away in A.D. 1708. There was thus an evolutionary process in Sikhism. Like Jainism and Buddhism, Sikhism was a revolt against neo-Brahmanism, but Sikhism also rejected the heterodox and atheistic faiths preached by Lord Mahavira and Lord Buddha.

Some scholars still maintain that Sikhism is a reform movement in Hinduism like Arya Samaj and Brahmo Samaj. They aver that all the Apostles of Sikh movement came from Hindu stock and were nurtured in Hindu tradition and lore. They merely revived the pure religion conceived by the *rishis* of yore. But a close study of the scriptures and Shastras of all the six systems of Hindu philosophy and five Bhakti cults, makes it clear that inspite of some similarities in the thought-content of the *Adi Granth* and the Hindu Shastras, there are a good number of basic differences in concepts.[4]

Dr. Trumpp says that Nanak remained a thorough Hindu according to all his views.[5] Malcolm is of the view that though Sikhism differs widely from the present worship of the Hindus, it has been th. ought to have considerable analogy to the pure and simple religion originally followed by that nation.[6] Gordon says, "Sikhism has had its roots solely in religious aspirations. It was a revolt against the tyranny of Brahmanism. On throwing off the yoke, Nanak and his disciples reverted instinctively to the old theistic creed of their ancestors".[7] Dr. Gokul Chand Narang has concluded that Sikhism is a phase of Hindu religious revival and has, in consequence, retained all essential features of real

21

Hinduism. But still he emphasises that "inspite of so many common features between Sikhism and ordinary Hinduism, there are certain points which distinguish Sikhism from Hinduism of the common masses".[8]

In his entry on "Sikhism" in "A Dictionary of Islam", Mr. Frederic Pincott has given another view. He says, "A careful investigation of early Sikh traditions points strongly to the conclusion that the religion of Nanak was really intended as a compromise between Hinduism and Muhammadanism, if it may not even be spoken of as the religion of a Muhammadan sect. . . . Nanak, though a Hindu by birth, came under Sufi influence, and was strongly attracted by the saintly demeanour of the *faqirs* who were thickly scattered over Northern India and swarmed in the Panjab. . . . Sikhism in its inception was intimately associated with Muhammadanism, and that it was intended as a means of bridging the gulf which separated the Hindu from the believers in the Prophet".[9]

Some Christian missionaries have tried to preach the idea that Sikhism was greatly influenced by Christianity. The word Isai[10] used for God has been misinterpreted as *Isa* or *Christ,* by the missionaries. Rev. E. Guilford in his booklet entitled *Sikhism* has tried to show the similarity in the following way: "One slok (couplet) from the Granth, which has a Christian colouring may be given here: "Je wad aap te vad teri daat, jin din kar ke kiti raat" (Translation: As Great as Thou Thyself art, so Great is Thy Gift—who having created the day, didst create the night). On reading this, the mind at once goes to the first chapter of Saint John's Gospel. There are many other sloks in the Granth which bear a remarkable resemblance to much that is found in the Gospels. This likeness led learned Indian Christian of the district of Gujrat to study the Granth closely, and the conclusion he came to was that Nanak was a convinced Christian, who taught, but in obscure language, the whole doctrine of the life of Christ, from his birth to his Ascension".[11]

The similarities in thought can be found here, there and elsewhere in various domains of knowledge because of the resembling circumstances in the lives of men, therefore it is not appropriate to deduce the impact of the one upon the other, unless there is direct involvement of movements. Guru Nanak Dev came in direct contact with Islamic personalities and institutions, therefore we find in his compositions his views about the Islamic doctrines. He has defined Islam in his own way. He has rejected the formalism and rituals in Islam.

# II

Various scholars have discussed the evolution of Sikh Religion keeping in view the contribution made by its Ten Masters, beginning with the birth of the first Divine Master, Guru Nanak Dev in A.D. 1469 and ending with the passing away of the Tenth Master, Guru Gobind Singh in A.D. 1708. This span of about 240 years is remarkable in Indian history. The rule of Lodhi dynasty declined and the Mughals gained supremacy in the sub-continent. In its relation to Sikhism, the period reflects the events of the lives of the Mughal emperors from Babur to Aurangzeb on the one hand and the religious teachings of Guru Nanak Dev and his successors on the other. Guru Gobind Singh wrote in his autobiography "Bachittar Natak": "The Supreme Ishvara Created side by side the houses of both Babur and Baba (Guru Nanak), the first symbolising the worldly grandeur, and the other, the spiritual excellence".[12]

While tracing the evolution of the Sikh Religion, some scholars have gone beyond the time and teachings of Guru Nanak Dev. In this sense, the origin of Sikhism goes back to Sant tradition of Northern India and farther goes back to India's antiquity. One such view has recently been expressed by W.H. McLeod in his book "The Evolution of Sikh Community". He says, "To Sikhs of all subsequent generations Guru Nanak is the founder of Sikh Religion. Of his importance there can be no doubt whatsoever, and it must also be acknowledged that in a certain sense he is legitimately described as a founder. The following that gathered around this man was certainly the original nucleus of the Sikh Panth and if we are to follow organisational lines in our movement back through history, we shall be able to proceed no further than this nucleus and the man. In another sense, however, the term "founder" is misleading, for it suggests that Guru Nanak originated not merely a group of followers but also a school of thought, or set of teachings. This can be accepted as true only in a highly qualified sense. If we place Guru Nanak with his own historical context, if we compare his teachings with those of other contemporary or earlier religious figures, we shall at once see that he stands firmly within a well-defined tradition. What Guru Nanak offers us is the clearest and most highly articulated expression of the *Nirguna Sampradaya*, the so-called Sant tradition of Northern India".[13]

This cleverly worded statement brings forth clearly the view that Guru Nanak Dev is the founder of Sikhism for the Sikhs only and for others Sikhism is an offshoot of the Sant tradition of Northern India, which had its roots in the Upanishadic age. On the surface of it the statement of Dr. McLeod appears logical for an ordinary reader, but, undoubtedly, there is a hidden sting in it. He is trying to minimise the significance of Sikhism as a distinct Religion and presents it only as an upsurge in the main stream of Sant tradition. He is doubtful about the position of Guru Nanak Dev as founder of the Sikh Religion, because, in a certain sense, the Guru can be legitimately described as a founder. His statement is most confusing for humanity at large.

Another foreigner, Dr. Gerald Barrier, has emphasised that Sikhism became a Religion only in the nineteenth century, and this was symbolised by the assertion, *Hum Hindu Nahin,* an expression of the Sikh Society to locate their religious History and hence, their own personal identity, outside the Hindu Matrix.[14]

The following questions have been raised by Ainslee T. Embree: "Was Nanak's role analogous on a smaller historical canvas, to that of the Buddha who is a *founder* in that he is a necessary part of the religious myths that provide a frame for doctrine, but whose actual historicity is irrelevant? Or was he like Jesus, whose historical existence is both necessary and relevant for believers, but whose actual biography cannot be recovered? The survey of historical studies suggest that Sikhism, like Christianity, is a creation of a believing community, and that while Guru Nanak's historicity is unquestioned, his reality resides in the necessity for the community's faith".[15]

Whereas the historicity of Buddha is said to be irrelevant, the historicity of Jesus and Guru Nanak Dev is unquestioned. The actual biography of Jesus, according to T. Embree cannot be recovered but what about the biography of Guru Nanak Dev? Guru Nanak Dev lived only five hundred years back, why should we doubt about the majority of incidents regarding his life found in early Sikh traditions, as has been done by Dr. McLeod in his book "Guru Nanak and the Sikh Religion"? Everything recorded about him in the Janamsakhis and other Sikh chronicles cannot be called a myth. The western scholars are going too far. They may even doubt his historicity. But they cannot dare to do it because of the available records, his compositions and memorials and more so, the line of

24

succession, which continued till the beginning of the eighteenth century in personal Guruship and in the form of *word* (i.e. *Guru Granth Sahib*) even to-day. There is a lot of symbolism in the Janamsakhis which cannot be understood by the western scholars unless they are saturated with the Indian wisdom.

The religion of Buddha is called Buddhism, the religion of Christ is known as Christianity. But the religion of Guru Nanak Dev is called Sikhism and not Nanakism or Nanakianity. This might have caused doubts in the minds of the western scholars regarding the origin of Sikhism, since the word 'Sikh' has its origin in the Sanskrit word 'Shishya', and the Guru-Shishya tradition is very old in India, which takes us back to the Upanishadic period. Even the Bhaktas (saints) belonging to the Sant tradition, namely Namdev, Kabir and Ravidas had large followings in the country. They were Gurus of their 'Shishyas' (disciples). But none of them found any distinct religion of their own. They have nowhere claimed their Panth as Sikh Panth. Their link with Sikh Panth as founded by Guru Nanak was formed only after the inclusion of their verses in the Guru Granth Sahib *(Adi Granth)* by Guru Arjan Dev, because of the identity of basic doctrines. This does not mean that Sikhism pre-existed in Namdev, Kabir or Ravidas, though these saints have been shown as great Bhaktas of the Lord in the compositions of the successors of Guru Nanak Dev.

The Upanishads composed by the *rishis* of yore have a close affinity of thought with the compositions of the poets of Sant tradition, including the poetry of the Sikh Gurus. Guru Nanak Dev seems to have studied the Upanishads. Guru Arjan Dev had studied many *Shastras* and *Smritis,* but that does not mean that Sikhism had anything to do with the ancient period of Indian culture. Some one may call the Sant tradition the revival of the religious fervour and thought of the ancient seers, but that cannot identify as a whole the new religion born under totally different circumstances.

### III

There is no denying the fact that a spiritual exercise of the centuries gives birth to a new religion. Guru Nanak Dev, the high-priest of Indian mysticism, whose mission culminated in due course from the second to

25

the tenth Nanak. He himself was the first missionary of his religion. He was, indeed, the founder of his mission and travelled not only throughout the length and breadth of the Indian sub-continent, but also in various countries abroad. He established *dharamsalas* (the centres for religious congregations), wherever he went and in several countries he is remembered with profound veneration and devotion even to-day. His mission was not confined to the frontiers of his home province, but, instead, it was universal. He met the votaries of all the existing religions of his time and discussed with them the salient features of his mission.

The western scholars only present doubts and conjectures, which suit their convictions and convenience. Doubts could even be expressed regarding the founder of Christianity. While describing the essential excellence of Christian Religion, Theodore Parker has recorded in his book "A Discourse of Matter pertaining to Religion" in 1877:

"Let us call the religious teachings of Jesus Christianity, it agrees generically with all other forms in this, that it is a Religion. Its peculiarity is not in its doctrine of One Infinite God, of the Immortality of Man, nor of future retribution. It is not in particular rules of morality, for precepts as true and beautiful may be found in Heathen writers, who give us the same view of Man's nature, duty and destination. The great doctrines of Christianity were known long before Jesus, for God did not leave man four thousand years unable to find out his plainest duty. There is no precept of Jesus, no real duty commended, no promises offered, no sanction held out, which cannot be paralleled by similar precepts in writers before him. The pure in heart saw God before as well as after him. Every imperfect form of religion was, more or less, an anticipation of Christianity. So far a man has real Religion, so far he has what is true in Christianity. By its light Zoroaster, Confucius, Pythagoras, Socrates, with many millions of holy men, walked in the early times of the world. By this they were cheered when their souls were bowed down, and they knew not which way to turn. They and their kindred, like Moses, were schoolmasters to prepare the world for Christianity; shadows of good things to come, one day springs from on high; the Bethlehem star announcing the Perfect Religion, which is to follow".[14]

26

Continuing his thesis Mr. Theodore Parker has concluded with the following remarks:

> "Notwithstanding the anticipation of the doctrines of Jesus centuries before him,—*Christianity was a new thing;* new in its spirit, proved new by the life it wakened in the world."

The same can be said about Sikhism. *IT WAS A NEW THING* founded by the Divine Master Guru Nanak Dev. His mission was new in its spirit and his Religion proved new by the life it wakened in the world. There is always an opposition for the new message given to the world by the founder and the Apostles of the new Religion. The reactionaries tried to malign Guru Nanak Dev and even raised their hands in order to stone him to death. Later on, the fifth and the ninth Gurus fell martyrs at the hands of fanatic rulers. The Tenth Master had to fight against the oppressor throughout his life.

The coming of Guru Nanak Dev and the birth of his new Religion had been foretold a long time before him by Vyasa in his *Bhavishya Purana.* He recorded that Nanak would take birth in the western part of the country and his followers would play a distinct role. Even if such a prediction may be considered dubious, we have other sources which clearly indicate the position of Guru Nanak Dev vis-a-vis the birth of Sikh Religion.

Bhai Gurdas, the great Sikh Theologian, who lived in the times of four Sikh Gurus, from the third to the sixth, and was scribe of the first recension of the *Adi Granth,* compiled by Guru Arjan Dev in A.D. 1604, wrote in his first Var that Guru Nanak Dev founded the pure Religion:

"Nanak nirmal Panth chalaya".[17]

In his compositions, he has mentioned several times the merits of a Sikh, which shows clearly that Sikhism had been established by that time. Guru Nanak Dev has been depicted as the Guru of the Gurus,[18] who had subdued the leaders of all the faiths during his wide travels.[19]

In the Var of Satta and Balwand, in Raga Ramkali of the *Guru Granth Sahib,* Balwand says, "Nanak has founded the (spiritual) kingdom in the citadel of Truth with powerful foundation":

"Nanak raj chalaya sach kot satani neev dai".[20]

The evidence of Bhai Gurdas and Balwand is both authentic and conclusive.

In the context of Guru-Sikh relation in Sikhism, a question arises about the Guru of Guru Nanak Dev. Persons ignorant about the Sikh tradition have very often blundered on this point. Several personalities have been claimed as his Guru, including Ramananda, Kabir, Ravidas and Baba Farid. Kabir and Ravidas are said to have met Guru Nanak Dev during his travels, but the Guru has neither made any mention of these saints in his compositions, nor of Ramananda and Baba Farid. The spiritual genealogy, of the Guru, of course can help us in tracing the origin of his faith, if ancient origin of Sikhism is claimed. Guru Nanak Dev has talked about the six Gurus i.e. Teachers of the six systems of Hindu philosophy, but he rejected all of them. Bhai Gurdas has said, "Nanak Vedi took birth in the Iron age and rejected all the six philosophies".[21] Guru Amar Das, the third Sikh Guru said, "Six philosophies are prevalent, but the philosophy of the Guru is unfathomable".[22] The distinct philosophy of the religion of Guru Nanak Dev is declared. The contemporary Yogis of Guru Nanak Dev questioned him during a spiritual discourse: "Who is your Guru, of whom you are the disciple?"[23] The Guru did not name any Guru of the day or any other personage of the mediaeval or ancient period, because none in the mortal frame could be his teacher. He replied immediately:

"The WORD is my Guru and my concentration is the disciple.[24]

In another hymn, Guru Nanak Dev clearly mentions the name of his Guru. "Nanak hath met that Guru, who is Supreme Brahman, Supreme Ishavara and Infinite".[25] Guru Gobind Singh has talked in the same strain, when he says:

He, Who is in the beginning and at the end, Consider him my only Guru.[26]

Thus the Omnipresent, Omnipotent and Omniscient Lord blessed Guru

28

Nanak Dev for the propagation of this New Faith. Bhai Gurdas has said: "Baba (Nanak) visited the region of Truth *(Sach Khand)* and received the Name of the Lord and modesty".[27] He, in turn, bequeathed them to his devotees.

## REFERENCES

1. T.M.P. Mahadevan: *Outlines of Hinduism*, Chetna Limited, Bombay, 1956.
2. Swami Nirvedananda: *Hinduism at a Glance*, Ramakrishna Mission, Calcutta, 1968.
3. P. Banerjee: *Early Indian Religions*, Vikas Publishing House, Delhi, 1973.
4. S.S. Kohli: *Sikh Ethics*, M/s Munshiram Manoharlal Publishers, New Delhi, 1975, See the Chapter "Justification of Sikh Ethics".
5. Dr. E. Trumpp: *The Adi Granth*, Munshiram Manoharlal Publishers, New Delhi, 1970.
6. John Malcolm: *Sketch of the Sikhs* included in *"The Sikh Religion"* Susil Gupta Pvt. Ltd., Calcutta, 1958.
7. John H. Gordon: *The Sikhs*, William Blackwood & Sons, Edinburgh, 1904.
8. Dr. Gokul Chand Narang: *Transformation of Sikhism*, New Book Society of India, New Delhi, 1963.
9. Thomas Patrick Hughes: *A Dictionary of Islam*, W.H. Alien & Co., London, 1885.
10. *bali bali jai prabh apune Isai, Adi Granth*, Maru M.5, p. 1072.
11. Rev. E. Guilford: *Sikhism in the non-Christian Religions series*, printed at Lay Reader Headquarters, Westminster, 1915.
12. Guru Gobind Singh: *Bachittar Natak*, Babe ke Babur ke dou, Ap kie Parmeshar sou
13. W.H. McLeod: *The Evolution of Sikh Community*, Oxford University Press, London, 1975.
14. Mark Juergensmeyer and N. Gerald Barrier: *Sikh Studies*, Berkeley Religious Studies series, 1974, See the article *"Comments: Locating Sikhism in Time and Place: A Problem for Historical Surveys"*

by Ainslir T. Embree

15. Ibid.
16. Theodore Parker: *A Discourse of Matters pertaining to Religion*. Trubner & Co., London, 1877.
17. Bhai Gurdas: Var 1, Pauri 45.
18. Bhai Gurdas: Var 3, Pauri 12.
19. Bhai Gurdas: Var 1, Pauri 34.
20. Satta and Balwand: Var Ramkali, Pauri 1, *Adi Granth*, p. 966.
21. Bhai Gurdas: Var 1, Pauri 41.
22. Guru Amar Das: *Adi Granth*, Asa, p. 360.
23. Guru Nanak Dev: *Siddh Goshta*, Ramkali, stanza 43.
24. Ibid., stanza 44.
25. Guru Nanak: *Adi Granth, Sorath*, p. 599. "Aprampar Parbrahm Parmesuru Nanak Guru milia soi jiu"
26. Guru Gobind Singh: *Chaupai* (Dasam Granth)
27. Bhai Gurdas: Var 1, Pauri 24.

# The Salient Features of Sikhism

The pivot of Sikh Thought is considered the Primary Sacred Formula (Mul Mantra), which occurs hundreds of times in the Guru Granth Sahib (Adi Granth), the scripture of the Sikhs. An enquiry into the nature of the Ultimate Reality takes us first of all to the study of this sacred formula. The very first word of this formula i.e. Ik Omkara is significant. It conveys the Unity of Brahman and also its two aspects i.e. the unmanifested (nirguna) and the manifested (Saguna). I quote here the text of the formula, giving its equivalent in English:

Ik Omkara (The One Omkara, the manifested as well as unmanifested Brahman) Satnam (His Name is Truth) Karta Purakh (A Purusha, who is the Creator) Nirbhau (without fear) Nirvair (without enmity) Akal Murat (A Being whom Death cannot assail) Ajuni (Unborn) Saibham (Self-existent) Gurprasad (With the grace of the Guru (preceptor))

The above formula presents the nature of the Ultimate Reality in a nutshell. This aphoristic text has to be elaborated from the hymns of the Adi Granth.

The figure One (Ik) in Ik Omkara denotes monotheism and Omkara (or Aumkara) denotes the Lord of the three faculties of creation, preservation and destruction. These faculties are represented by the gods of the Hindu Trinity viz., Brahma, Vishnu and Shiva. According to Guru Nanak, these gods are the product of maya (Illusion, Unreality), therefore they cannot see or realise Brahman, the Omnipotent, Omnipresent and Omniscient. They are born entities, therefore they are doomed to die. The Lord Himself is Unborn, Ever-existent (Sat), eternal and Immortal. He is self-existent (svayyam-bhu). Sikhism, thus, has no belief in gods or goddesses. God of Sikhism is One and only One, without a second. He is

31

above all relations; he has no consort, no brother and no son. Since there is none equal to Him, he is without any fear and enmity. He is always Gracious, Generous and Benevolent. He is never revengeful. Since He is Unborn and does not enter a womb, Sikhism has no belief in incarnations. Since God is without any form, colour, mark or lineage, therefore He can not be established or installed as an idol or image. He pervades throughout His creation. He is non-spacial and non-temporal. The souls are His part and parcel like the rays of the sun or the drops of the ocean. They emanate from Him and ultimately merge in Him. His laws (Hukm) prevail everywhere. There are physical laws, moral laws and spiritual laws. The souls adopt bodies according to their actions (karmas) and experience transmigration. The release is obtained by following a religious discipline through the spiritual preceptor (Guru). One meets the Guru by the Grace of the Lord and meets the Lord by the Grace of the Guru.

The discipline of the Guru regarding the quest for and unification with the Ultimate Reality has been given the names of Sahaja Yoga, Surt-Shabad Yoga and Nam Yoga. The Yoga of the Guru Granth Sahib (Adi Granth) is an amalgam of Bhakti Yoga (union through devotion), Karma Yoga (union through action), and Gyan Yoga (union through knowledge). It is neither Raja Yoga of Patanjali nor Hath-Yoga of Gorakhnath nor Kundalini Yoga. It is an upward flight from the region of piety (Dharam Khand) to the region of Truth (Sach Khand). The three intervening regions are the region of knowledge (Gyan Khand), the region of effort (Saram Khand) and the region of Grace (Karam Khand). Throughout his journey, the seeker is absorbed in devotion (Bhakti), remembrance of the Name of the Lord in the company of saintly persons, in whom the spirit of the Guru resides. Thus there is a spiritual ascent towards TRUTH or God, in which the seeker assimilates devotion, action and knowledge and attains the Grace of the Lord. The main actions of a Sikh (seeker) are the absorption in his work, company of good people and assimilation of godly qualities. God is Truth and devoid of fear and enmity. The seeker has to be truthful and without any fear and enmity. Without the qualities there can be no devotion. Without staunch faith, there can be no quest. The body is the temple of God, which must be kept clean, both outwardly and inwardly. The inward cleanliness comes through gradual practice of virtues and shedding away of vices. The principle vices are lust, anger, greed, attachment and ego. The principle virtues are celibacy, mercy, toleration, contentment, devotion to duty and modesty. Our body is the microcosm and only through this medium, we can see the Lord of the macrocosm through the control of the senses as ordained by the Guru. The state of *Sahaj*, the last reach of human experience will be realised by the devotee.

The *Adi Granth*, the scripture of the Sikhs, is the latest sacred book of Asia. It holds a unique position among the scriptures of the world. It was given the status of the Guru (preceptor) by the tenth and the last Sikh Guru, Guru Gobind Singh in A.D. 1708, thereby ending the line of personal Guruship. The *Adi Granth* thus became *Guru Granth Sahib*. It contains the *bani* of the Sikh Gurus and the radical saints of the Bhakti Movement. Besides the hymns of the first, second, third, fourth, fifth and ninth Sikh Gurus, it consists of the verses of some prominent Indian saints including those of Jaidev of Bengal (twelfth century), Sheikh Baba Farid of West Panjab (12th-13th century), Namdev and Trilochan of Maharashtra (14the century) and Kabir and Ravidas of Utar Pradesh (15th century). These compositions manifest synthesis of Indian thought, an exposition of the ideal life of an individual and society and a consummation of Indian culture. Although the path of life enunciated by the Sikh Gurus and the saints of the *Adi Granth* is the product of a definite period of Indian history, its tenets and beliefs belong to all times; its approach is universal.

Sikhism rejects asceticism and lays stress on the life of a householder. It is the religion of activity, not only in the world, in which we are born, but also in the inner spiritual world. We have been sent into the field of action; its renunciation will be a cowardly act. God does not live away from humanity and the world of *Jivas*. The Lord resides in the heart of every being and he who runs away from humanity causes the displeasure of the Lord, who lives in humanity. The Sikh dictum *"Kirt Karo, Wand Chhakko ate Nam Jappo"* (Work for a living, share your earnings with the needy and remember the Name of the Lord) gives us an insight into the life of a Sikh. For him work is worship. He has to work for the maintenance of his family, but he has also been enjoined to contribute generously for the deserving needy according to his means. Over and above this, he has also to attend to his spiritual needs. Guru Nanak Dev scolded the Yogis for having gone into the seclusion of the forests and mountains, while their services were badly needed for the suffering humanity. In his hymns the Guru has allegorically talked about the people

33

of the working class and has decried those who shun work and become parasites on society. Out of the four stages of life viz. Brahmcharya, Grahasthya, Vanaprastha and Sannyasa, the Guru rejected the first and the last two, giving preference only to the life of a householder. For him, only those people tread on the path of God, who work hard for sustaining themselves and their families and even give something for the welfare of the needy from their savings.

Sikhism rejects all formalism and ritualism and lays emphasis on the adoption of the ethical qualities. Out of the three parts of the Vedas i.e. *Karma Kanda, Upasana Kanda* and *Gyan Kanda,* Sikhism accepts only the *Gyan Kanda.* There is no priestly class in Sikhism. The devoted and learned Sikhs perform the services in the Sikh temples. The works enjoined by *Karma Kanda* and *Upasana Kanda* create ego in the minds of those, who perform them, therefore the Sikh Gurus and the radical saints have raised their voice against them.

Sikhism insists on poise and balance in life, equal stress on the physical and spiritual well-being of individual and society and a balanced combination of devotion, action and knowledge. Out of the four signifi-cant values of human life viz. *Dharma* (duty or virtue), *Artha* (wealth), *Kama* (pleasure or enjoyment) and *Moksha* (emancipation) the three ends of human action viz *Kama, Artha* and *Dharma* are inter-dependent. While *Moksha* or final emancipation is the highest end, because with its achievement all the sufferings cease and the state of supreme bliss is attained, *Dharma* is the basis of a great culture, because it leads towards virtuous life. It signifies the code of conduct formulated by the sages, seers and founders of religions. *Dharma,* according to Sikhism is the Power which sustains the earth in the proper place and supports the heavens without columns. A balanced combination of Dharma, Kama and Artha is necessary for the attainment of *Moksha.*

Sikhism preaches Fatherhood of God and brotherhood of man. It rejects all barriers and prejudices of caste, colour and birth and lays emphasis on equal status of man and woman in society. It speaks against all types of exploitation. The division of society into *varnas* (castes) was condemned by the Gurus and Saints. The *Brahmins* considered them-selves belonging to a distinct class and claimed highest prerogatives because of their birth. They alongwith *Kshatriyas* and *Vaishyas* were called dvijas (twice-born). The *Shudras* were meant to serve the *dvijas,* especially Brahmins. They were untouchables in the society. Kabir lashed out at the Brahmin: "If thou art born of a Brahmin-woman, why didst thou not come into the world through another path?" He said further, "How are you a Brahmin? and How am I a Shudra? How am I the blood and how are you the milk?" Guru Nanak Dev said, "No one asks for the caste and birth in the home of the True Lord. . . . The caste and honour are determined by the deeds." The tenth Master, Guru Gobind Singh said, "They have the same eyes, the same ears, the same bodies and the same habits and are composed of the same four elements." Then how they are different from each other? They are the sons of the same father. The caste, birth or colour cannot make one superior or inferior.

Woman is the most significant part of the society. She gives birth to the greatest individuals of the society. Therefore she should receive the utmost reverence. She is not only the better-half, she is also a gate for emancipation. As a daughter, mother, sister and wife, she should receive the due respect. She has equal rights in the society. The Sikh Gurus believed like Plato that there is to be no sex-barrier of any kind in the community, not even in education; the girl should have the same opportunities as the boy. Why a widow should not be allowed to re-marry? Why a woman be burnt to ashes with the dead? Guru Amar Das spoke severely against the custom of *Sati*. The woman has the same soul as the man and she has an equal right to grow spiritually, equal right to attend religious congregations and recite divine hymns in the temples. Polygamy is a sin. "One man and one wife" is the golden principle.

Sikhism is a Universal Religion. It rises above the restraints regarding food, clothing etc. It speaks against the use of drugs and intoxicants. That food is debarred, which makes the individual insane. It talks about the basic needs of an individual i.e. food, shelter and clothing and lays a great responsibility on the State regarding their provision. The State should be democratic and should work for the well-being and prosperity of individual and society. According to Guru Nanak Dev: when the king forgets his duties and indulges in self-gratification, his people are sure to revolt against him. His sons will be thrown into the streets, where they will not be able to get even a morsel of food. The reign of only those kings will be durable, who follow the democratic ideals. When the king becomes ferocious like a lion, his servants also become corrupt. The king got the lion's share of the booty and the remainder was licked by the

35

corrupt officials. He has to see that there is economic stability in the State. He should not resort to heavy taxation for his personal purse, but instead should charge only reasonable revenues, which may be sufficient for an efficient working of the State. It is the duty of the king to see that the basic needs of his subjects with regard to food, shelter and clothing may be fulfilled.

Sikhism advocates the excellence and utility of human life, the necessity of education, true preceptor and truthful living, the building of character, the inculcation of love, truth, contentment, humility and the achievement of spiritual greatness by following the path enunciated by the preceptor. The seeker has to concentrate on the Name of the Lord or the Word given by the Guru. The union with the Lord through His Name is known as *Surt-Shabad Yoga*. This Yoga purifies the mind and intellect of the disciple. The world is diseased and the Name of the Lord is the only remedy. The Name-culture keeps the disciple unaffected by maya, just as the lotus remains over and above the surface of water. There are two methods of the remembrance of the Name: by tongue and by breath. The discipline of the Guru requires the disciple to perform his worldly duties alongwith his spiritual progress; he has not to become a one-sided personality. He has to remain alert on all the three planes i.e. physical, mental and spiritual. The continuous repetition of the Name gradually brings a stage when the Name is repeated without effort in any posture or state, whether sitting or standing, awaking or sleeping. A stage comes in the life of a fully enlightened disciple, when there occurs the repetition of the Name through every pore of the body. That is the stage of perfection. The seeker is fully conscious of all the phenomena around him. He becomes a *Jivan-Mukta* having cut down all the knots of bondage, while living in the world. The gradual development on the spiritual plane takes place in the company of enlightened disciples (*Gurmukh*, Sadh, Sant). This company is known as *Satsang* or the holy congregation. Music *(Kirtan)* plays a significant part at such congregations, where the hymns of the Gurus and saints contained in the *Adi Granth* are sung individually and in chorus. The main emphasis is on devotion through love *(Prema Bhakti)*, Listening attentively to the scripture (Shravana), reflection on the contents of the scripture with faith (manan) and intellectual conviction and concentration *(niddhyasana)* lead to the true knowledge of God *(Brahm Gyan)*.

36

A Significant feature of Sikhism is its view regarding the extent of cosmos. Guru Nanak did not accept the idea of the delimitation of the universe expressed by the contemporary religions. He argued with the theologians of his day that the "Creation of the Infinite Lord cannot be finite." He said, "There are lakhs of nether-worlds and lakhs of skies. Even the Vedas declare unanimously that the ends of creation cannot be determined. The eighteen thousand *Shalokas* of *Bhagavata Purana* and the Muslim scriptures say that there is only One Reality. He is unaccountable. Those who make an account of His creation destroy themselves. The Lord is great, He alone knows His greatness." Modern scientist like Hoyle and Gold believe that the universe is expanding and with regard to time and space, it is infinite. The same view was held by Guru Nanak about five centuries earlier. Modern scientists believe in the infinity of space and the existence of millions of solar systems. Guru Nanak Dev speaks in the same strain: "There is no end to His creation. . . . Nobody can know His limits, the more we see, the more they extend . . . only He knows His greatness." Guru Arjan Dev speaks of crores of upper regions and universes: "There are crores of divisions of organic production. There are crores of regions. There are crores of skies and universes." In the Hindu Trinity, Brahma is the creator, but Guru Arjan Dev speaks about millions of Brahmas engaged by the Infinite Lord, who is the Master of millions of universes.

For a Sikh, the major instructions of the Guru are: the remembrance of the Name of the Lord, the practice of godly qualities in life and total surrender to the Guru. The initiation ceremony in Sikhism is called *Amrit Chhakna* (drinking of the water of immortality) in which the miracle of the Name of the Lord works. This miracle changed the shape of events in the history of India. For an initiated Sikh (or a Singh) there are four taboos i.e. shaving or cutting of hair, adopting slavish mentality, using intoxicants and adultery and fornication. A Sikh is enjoined to contribute *daswandh* or one-tenth of his earnings for the common good. The deserving and needy are to be given help out of this fund. The common kitchen *(Langar)* started with the contribution from the common fund was a general feature of the Sikh Movement since the times of the Gurus. It created a sense of equality among the members of Sikh brotherhood. But this common kitchen is not meant for needy Sikhs only; it has to remain open for all. In the common kitchen a Brahmin sits side by side with a Shudra, a king with the lowliest of the subjects, on the same carpet. This creates confidence among the workers of all types regarding the respect of their profession. The persons of higher rank are emptied of their ego and they consider themselves as public servants, meant for the service of common people. All of them are unified in a bond of brotherhood. The sisters have an equal status with their brothers. They help in the kitchen, but at the time of distribution of meals, they sit and enjoy meals with their brethren. The Sikh society has a universal outlook and discards all types of parochialism. Its motto is SERVICE and its slogan is EXCELSIOR.

# Constant Unity of Sikh Thought

It has often been expressed by various scholars and historians that with the passage of time, even in the lives of the Sikh Gurus, a great change occured in the Sikh Movement. From Guru Nanak Dev to the fifth Guru, Guru Arjan Dev, the movement was peaceful, but the change occured when the sixth Guru, Guru Hargobind became the Pontiff, after the martyrdom of his father. He wore not only one sword, but two swords, those of *miri* (worldly grandeur) and *piri* (spiritual grandeur). He fought several battles with the Mughal army. The seventh, eighth and ninth Gurus were peaceful, but the tenth Guru, not only wielded the sword, after the martyrdom of his father, but also gave birth to Khalsa, a brotherhood of warriors. These scholars argue that Guru Nanak Dev, the founder of the faith never thought of anything else than the purity and saintliness in life, but with the sword-wielding Gurus and the Khalsa, the movement turned into a brotherhood of warriors and soldiers.

Sir Jadunath Sarkar in his book "History of Aurangzeb" asserts that the Sikhs were organised by Guru Gobind Singh "to suit a special purpose". He is of the view that the Guru made the human energy of the Sikhs flow from all sides into one particular channel only, so much so that the Sikhs ceased to be full, free men. Their spiritual unity was converted into a means of worldly success. The Guru "dwarfed the unity of a religious sect into an instrument of political advancement. As a consequence, according to Sarkar, the Sikhs who had been advancing for centuries to be true men, suddenly stopped short and became mere soldiers.

Toynbee, the celebrated modern historian, in his book "A Study of History" (Vol.VII) says that an outstanding example of self-stultification through resort to force was presented in Hindu history by Sikhism. According to him Sikhism had started by practising fraternity as a corollary to its preaching of monotheism, but it went astray through

39

allowing itself to become the sectarian faith of militant founders of a successor state of the Mughal Raj. He adds further that it had come eventually to be little more than the distinctive mark of a community that had virtually become another Hindu caste.

In his book "Man's Religions", John B. Noss remarks that Nanak's creed and practice were distinctly quietistic, and yet it was the singular faith of the religion he established to change with the years into a vigorously activist political faith. According to him various influences were to provide a notable modification of this code of philanthropy, honesty, and holiness, and introduce in full strength a military ardor, a self-dedication to the arbitrament of the sword, that is a unique and in some respects a distressing story.

Dr. Trumpp in his "Introduction to the Adi Granth" says, "Guru Arjan's death is the great turning point in the development of the Sikh Community, as from that time the struggle commenced that changed the entire character of the reformatory religious movement."

In his entry on *Sikhism* in "A Dictionary of Islam", edited by T.P. Hughes, Frederic Pincott has made the following remarks about Guru Gobind Singh, "He was brought up under Hindu guidance, and became a staunch devotee of the goddess Durga; and by his pronounced preference for Hinduism, he caused a division in the Sikh Community. He introduced several important changes into the constitution of Sikh society. The chief among these was the establishment of the Khalsa, by which he bound his disciples into an army, conferred upon each of them the name Singh, or lion. He freely admitted all castes to the ranks of his army and laboured more earnestly over their military than over their religious discipline. The nature of the changes which Gobind Singh effected in the fraternity is best known by the fact that the special followers of Nanak personally separated themselves from him, and formed a community of their own, rejecting the title of Singh. In other words, they preferred the religious to the military idea.

Most recently, Dr. W.H. Mcleod has discerned the change taking place in the Sikh Movement from the time of the third Guru, Guru Amar Das. He has drawn our attention to the declaration of Guru Nanak Dev that there was only one *tirath* (Pilgrim-station) for the true devotee and that was within his own heart. According to Dr. Mcleod, this declaration has been spurned by Guru Amar Das by providing a new pilgrim-centre to the

40

community. In the words of Dr. Mcleod "Not only did he provide this new pilgrimage centre, but also distinctive festival days, distinctive rituals, and a collection of sacred writings. Guru Nanak had rejected all of these. Guru Amar Das, in different and more difficult circumstances, is compelled to return to them".

According to Dr. Mcleod, the militancy in the Sikh Movement from the time of Guru Hargobind was due to the Jat influx in the community. He feels that the penetration of the Jats within the Sikh fold began very early, because the area in which the first five Gurus lived was particularly a Jat area. In his view, "the Jat incursion was of considerable importance in the evolution of the community, particularly for the developments which took place during the seventeenth and eighteenth centuries." He has commented further that the growth of militancy within the Panth must be traced primarily to the impact of Jat cultural patterns and to economic problems which prompted a militant response.

The thoughts of a few historians and scholars, given above, contain the following important points:

1. The spiritual unity was converted by Guru Gobind Singh into a means of worldly success. He dwarfed the unity into an instrument of political advancement.

2. The Sikh Movement went astray by allowing itself to become the sectarian faith of militant founders.

3. The faith of Guru Nanak changed with the years into a vigorously activist political faith. Thee was a notable modification in the code of philanthropy, honesty and holiness.

4. After the death of Guru Arjan Dev, the struggle commenced, which changed the entire character of the reformatory religious movement.

5. As a consequence of the changes effected by Guru Gobind Singh, the special followers of Guru Nanak Dev personally separated themselves from him and formed a community of their own, rejecting the title of Singh.

6. The change in the Sikh Movement took place from the time of Guru Amar Das. He provided a new pilgrim-centre, distinctive festival days, distinctive rituals and a collection of sacred writings, which had been rejected by Guru Nanak Dev.

7. The militancy in the Sikh Movement from the time of Guru Hargobind was due to the Jat influx in the Community.

The above statements of historians and scholars expressing a great change in the Sikh Movement, need thorough investigation. There is a great misrepresentation of facts. The evolution of the Sikh community has been misinterpreted. This shows the lack of understanding of the Sikh thought, which could not be visualised in the right perspective. In this short essay it is our endeavour to clarify the above-mentioned misstatements.

The fact is that the spiritual unity had never been impaired. The spirit of the founder Guru worked within all the successive Gurus. It is recorded in the Var of Satta and Balwand in the *Adi Granth* that with each Guru, Guru Nanak changed his body. The spirit of Guru Nanak Dev worked in each Guru, therefore each succeeding Guru was Guru Nanak himself and as a proof he bore the seal of "Nanak". Do we not find the name of "Nanak" in the verses of the second, third, fourth, fifth and ninth Guru in Guru Granth Sahib (the Adi Granth)? Balwand says, "Guru Nanak Dev bestowed the mark of Guruship on Lehna, who had the same light and the same method; it was the primal Guru who had changed the body". In the same poem, it is written about the third Guru Amar Das and the fourth Guru Ram Das: "Guru Nanak, the Enlightener, appeared in the form of Amar Das. . . . The following was astonished to see Guru Nanak Dev's canopy over the head of Guru Amar Das. The third Guru obtained the same throne and the same court. . . . Hail, hail, O Guru Ram Das, the Lord Who has created you, has Decked you. . . . You are Nanak, you are Lehna and you are Amar Das." Thus all the Sikh Gurus are one, there is no difference between them. The same fact has been conveyed by Bhai Gurdas in his first Var. He says, "It was during his lifetime that Guru Nanak Dev bestowed Guruship on Lehna. Guru Nanak transformed himself into Angad by infusing his light in him. . . . Guru Angad Dev had the same mark, the same canopy over his head and sat on the same throne, on which Guru Nanak Dev had sat earlier. He had the same seal of Guru Nanak Dev in his hand and in this way the sovereignty of Guru Angad Dev was proclaimed. . . . The gift obtained by Lehna from Guru Nanak Dev had to be given to Amar Das. The bestowal of the gift and light depends on the blessings of the Lord. The gift to be given is pre-destined; it comes

42

to the house of one to whom it belongs. There sat the Sodhi king Ram Das, addressed as the True Guru. . . . Then the Guruship came in the house of Arjan, who was called Guru, though he was the real son (of the previous Pontiff). . . . Then Arjan transformed himself and decked in the form of Hargobind. . . ".

The oneness and the unity of the Gurus has also been highlighted by Guru Gobind Singh in his autobiography entitled *Bachittar Natak*. He says, "Nanak transformed himself to Angad and spread Dharma in the world. He was called Amar Das in the next transformation. A lamp was lighted from the lamp. When the opportune time came for the boon, then the Guru was called Ram Das. He was bestowed upon the old boon, when Amar Das departed for the heavens. Sri Nanak was recognised in Angad and Angad in Amar Das. Amar Das was called Ram Das; only the saints knew it and the fools did not. The people on the whole considered them as separate ones, but there were few who recognised them as one and the same. Those who recognised them as One, they were successful on the spiritual plane. Without recognition, there was no success. When Ram Das was merged in the Lord, the Guruship was bestowed upon Arjan. When he left for the abode of the Lord, Hargobind was seated on his throne. When Hargobind left for the abode of the Lord, Har Rai was seated in his place. Har Krishan (the next Guru) was his son. After him, Tegh Bahadur became the Guru. He protected the forehead mark and the sacred thread (of the Hindus) which marked a great event in the Iron age. For the sake of saints, he laid down his head without even a sigh. For the sake of Dharma, he sacrificed himself; he laid down his head, but not his creed.

This fact of oneness and unity permeated in the hearts of the Sikhs, with such intensity that it was mentioned in the famous Muslim chronicle *"Dabistan-i-Mazahib"* in the following words: "The Sikhs say that when Nanak left his body, he absorbed himself in Guru Angad, who was his most devoted disciple, and that Guru Angad is Nanak himself. After that, at the time of his death, Guru Angad entered into the body of Amar Das. He in the same manner occupied a place in the body of Ram Das, and Ram Das in the same way got united with Arjan. . . . They say that whoever does not acknowledge Guru Arjan to be the very self of Baba Nanak becomes a non-believer. . . ". This Persian Book was written about a century after Guru Nanak Dev.

This oneness and the unity of spirit can be further elaborated in the unity of Thought on the basis of the compositions of the Sikh Gurus. Guru Nanak Dev considered our earth as the abode of *Dharma*, wherein the initiate or the devotee has to practise *Dharma*. *Dharma*, according to the Sanskrit lexicon, connotes religious or moral discipline of piety and righteousness. Dharma is the foundation, on which the spiritual excellence can be achieved. Guru Nanak Dev said, "'One should remain firm on truth' is the only Dharma". (p.1188, Basant M.1). The Guru has thus identified Dharma with truth. The same idea has been given by Guru Arjan Dev, when he said, "One should destroy the falsehood and remain firm on Dharma" (p.518, Var Gujri M.5). He also said, "Do not delay the acts of Dharma, let there be delay in sinful act" (p.1354, Sahaskriti Shlokas M.5). Guru Gobind Singh categorically says that he had been sent by the Lord in the world for the spread of Dharma. He says, "I have come for this work in the world and my Gurudeva has sent me to propagate Dharma. The Lord has asked me to spread Dharma and vanquish the tyrants and evil-minded persons. The saints should comprehend this in their minds that I have taken birth to spread Dharma, protect saints and root out tyrants and evil-minded persons. (*Bachittar Natak*, Section VI). These words of the tenth Guru amply prove that his whole struggle was aimed at the spread of piety and righteousness. The Lord whom he cherished in word and spirit appeared to him as a deadly weapon for tyrants and evil-minded persons. He considered the sword as a symbol of Almighty, therefore he bowed to it in reverence. The use of the sword was made only to protect the lowly and weak and punish the unjust. His "Zafarnama" (Epistle of Victory), written to Aurangzeb, will always inspire his followers. The sowrd was meant to defend and not to offend. He said, "If all the other methods fail for reconciliation, it is appropriate to take up the sword in hand." Guru Hargobind, the sixth Sikh Guru wore the two swords of *miri* and *piri*, symbolising the worldly and spiritual grandeur respectively. These swords passed on through his son Guru Tegh Bahadur to his grandson Guru Gobind Singh. Both these swords arose from both the ends of Dharma. The sword of *Piri* (spirituality) was apparent in the House of Guru Nanak Dev and his successors, but the sword of *Miri*, though latent in earlier Gurus, became manifest after the martyrdom of the fifth Guru, Guru Arjan Dev and became doubly sharp and lustrous with the birth of the Khalsa. The Khalsa was latent in the *Sat*

44

*Sangat* founded by Guru Nanak Dev. Its bravery and chivalry was latent in Guru Arjan Dev's mace of humility and the double-edged sword of modesty (p.628, Sorath M.5). Guru Nanak Dev had said, "If God Wills, He Brandishes the Sword to cut the head of the enemy" (p.145, Var Majh M.1). That Sword of Dharma was put in the hands of Guru Hargobind and Guru Gobind Singh. Having been ignorant of the Sikh Thought, modern historians and scholars have misunderstood the implication of the use of Sword by the Sikh Gurus and the Khalsa.

Bhai Gurdas wrote about Guru Hargobind: "He, the warrior Guru, is the destroyer of the armies, a great hero and a great philanthropist." (Var I) Bhai Gurdas Singh, a contemporary poet, wrote about Guru Gobind Singh: "A Unique person was born, the unparalleled hero. Hail, hail, O Gobind Singh, You are the Guru as well as the disciple". (Var). How could such immaculate personalities be said to have turned away from the path of purity and philanthropy? Whereas a couplet in the Shlokas of Kabir presents the crux of Guru Nanak's Thought in the following words: "Do all the work with your hands and feet, but keep the mind absorbed in the Lord" (p.1376, Shalok Kabir) the following thought of Guru Gobind Singh is quite identical with the above thought: "Blessed is his life in the world, who has the Name of the Lord in his mouth and thinks of the battle (of righteousness) in his heart. The mortal body will not last long. He should embark the raft of the Lord's Praises in order to be crossed across the ocean of the world. He should make this body the abode of forbearance, illumining his intellect like a lamp. He should take the broom-stick of knowledge in his hand and sweep away the rubbish of cowardice." (The last stanza of *Krishnavatara*).

The religion of Guru Nanak Dev is the religion of love. Guru Nanak Dev said, "Valueless is the pride of caste and name. The Lord Gives Shade to all" (p.83, Var Sri Rag M.4, Shalok M.1). The Guru had firm belief in universal brotherhood. Love is a godly quality and with Love one feels the nearness of God. Guru Amar Das said, "The world is burning, Save it, O Lord, Be Merciful on it. Emancipate it through any Door, where it can be saved." (p.853, Var Bilawal M.4, Shalok M.3). The Guru focusses his attention on the humanity as a whole. Guru Arjan Dev said, "I have befriended all; none is inimical towards me." (p.671, Dhanasari M.5). And Guru Gobind Singh said, "Recognise the unity in all the humanity.... All the humans have the same eyes, the same ears, the same

45

body the same nature and the same combination of air, earth, fire and water." (Akal Ustat – Dasam Granth). The Guru firmly believed in equality and fraternity. Without the knowledge of the tenets of the Sikh Gurus, the historians and scholars have not been able to consider their lives and doctrines in right perspective. The Gurus had no political ambition and no worldly aspirations. They were religious leaders. The religion was the foundation of all their activities. They wanted the spiritual development of the populace and any movement that stood in the way of spiritual development of the populace and any movement that stood in the way of spiritual development was not liked by them. The ferocious and mad tyrants, pouncing on the helpless populace, had to be dealt with in a befitting manner by the sword of Dharma. In the words of Guru Nanak Dev:

There can be no displeasure, if a powerful person kills a powerful person,

But if a powerful lion falls upon a flock of sheep, or a herd of cattle, then the Master must answer. (p.360, Asa M.1).

Dr. Mcleod discerns the change coming in the Sikh Movement from the time of the third Sikh Guru, Guru Amar Das. This, according to him, is based on two factors. The first is regarding the *tirtha* (pilgrim station) built by the Guru in violation of the sayings of the first Guru, who had said, "My *tirtha* is the Name of the Lord". (p.687, Dhanasari M.1). We do not know how Dr. Mcleod has concluded that the *tirtha* of Guru Amar Das was Baoli Sahib and not the Name of the Lord? The Guru himself says, "That is the true place of pilgrimage, where one bathes in the Pool of Truth; the Lord Himself makes the *Gurmukh* (the disciplined devotee) realise this. The Word of the Guru awards the merit of bathing at the sixty-eight *tirthas* in which the dirt is washed off." (p.753, Suhi M.3). Thus for Guru Amar Das also, like Guru Nanak Dev, the real Tirtha is the Word of the Guru or the Name of the Lord. How can a foreign missionary, who boasts of using the most scientific methodology for his conclusions, know the real spirit of Sikhism, without delving deep into the compositions of the Gurus. Another factor which he mentions for the change in the Sikh Movement is the Jat influx in the community. Dr. Mcleod knows full well that Sikhism is antagonistic towards caste system. None of the castes

46

attracted any of the Gurus. Guru Nanak Dev had said, "In the House of the Lord (Truth), no one will ask you about your caste or birth. The deeds done by a person constitute his caste and merit." (p.1330, Prabhati M.1). Undoubtedly, the first five Gurus lived in an area, where the Jats were in majority, but the following of the Gurus was not limited to these areas. Their Sikhs were spread far and wide, not only in India, but in foreign countries as well, because Guru Nanak Dev had made extensive journeys in and out of India. Dr. Mcleod has very cleverly manipulated the issue of Khatri culture and Jat culture, which has no relevance in the evolution of the Sikh Movement. The missionary zeal lurking in his mind seems to be the cause of raking up the above issue, with the secret design of creating a cleavage among the Sikhs on caste basis. All the Sikhs were ready to sacrifice their lives for their Gurus, whether they were Khatris or Jats, whether they were Udasis or householders, whether they were men or women. The service of the Guru is dear to the Sikhs of all shades. The following statement of Dr. Mcleod is totally a misrepresentation of facts: "The growth of militancy within the Panth must be traced primarily to the impact of Jat cultural patterns and to economic problems, which prompted a militant response." (The Evolution of the Sikh Community, pp.12-13). In ordinary course of life, the individual may falter, but in the collective will of the community, which may manifest itself in the form of the holy congregation or the common kitchen, a Sikh is a Sikh and nothing else and everything in his possession, his body, mind and wealth, all belong to the Guru.

The Sikh society is a society of householders, a society of the saints, soldiers and scholars. Each Sikh is an amalgam of *Gyan* (knowledge), *Karma* (action) and *Bhakti* (devotion). *Bhakti* makes him a saint, *karma* a soldier and *Gyan* a scholar. Three jewels of *Kirt karna* (doing work), *wand chhakna* (sharing one's earning with the deserving and needy) and *Nam japna* (remembrance of the Name of the Lord) enlighten the path of his life. He faithfully practices the precept and discipline ordained by the Gurus. The discipline of the Gurus is one and the same. For him the discipline ordained by Guru Gobind Singh is not different from that of Guru Nanak Dev, the founder Guru. The discipline, in reality, concerns the inner self. In this respect, there is no difference between a Sahajdhari Sikh (an easygoing Sikh) and the Khalsa. The outer garb of the Khalsa is a manifestation of the inner discipline. The Khalsa wields the sword of

Dharma and retains the Complete Image of the Lord. The Khalsa is the martial unit of the Sikhs, specially created to fight against injustice and to protect the oppressed and suppressed ones.

Summing up the thought-content of this article, I wish to quote a passage from the article entitled "Guru Nanak and His Age", published by Sahitya Akademi, New Delhi, in its book "Guru Nanak—A Homage" and written by Shri A.R. Deshpande:

"Though, historically speaking, the age of Guru Nanak seems to have extended only till the tenth Guru Gobind Singh, its ideological influence continues till this day. Some historians seem to opine that Guru Nanak's original high concepts of religion were set on decline when the later Gurus introduced militarism into it, and led the Sikhs to ambitions of a political nature. It is difficult to agree wholly with such view. The course of Guru Nanak's Sikhism was turned that way by the need of survival in a wholly hostile atmosphere and not by political opportunism. Taking stock of the situations before and after Guru Nanak, one can say with a sense of pride and confidence that the age of Guru Nanak restored religion to its pristine simplicity and brought amelioration to the followers of contending religions. It built up confidence in the people and made it possible for them to live a valorous life of dignity and honour.... This the age of Guru Nanak accomplished, not only in Punjab, but in the whole of India."

# Contribution of Sikh Religion and Culture Towards Human Uplift

Sikhism is the youngest of the world religions. Its founder, Guru Nanak, was born in A.D. 1469. For about twenty years, he travelled extensively in various parts of the world, visiting especially the major religious centres of all the contemporary religions and preaching his gospel. In foreign lands, he was an Indian ambassador, with a difference. In the past, several Hindu and Buddhist sages and savants had gone abroad and had founded a 'Greater India' out of their country. They had taken with them the great Indian heritage concerned with their religious culture and brought several countries in the fold of their respective religions. But Guru Nanak had an original religious culture in view, of which he was the first preacher and missionary. He was an original thinker and a path-setter. He was wide awake to the prevailing conditions. At some places he won approbation for his message, while at others there were antagonistic, hostile forces. During his lifetime, he created a band of zealous followers not only in India, but in several countries abroad. After his passing away, he was succeeded by nine spiritual descendents, who made significant contribution in building up a strong base for this new faith. The last Guru, Guru Gobind Singh, created the *Khalsa*, the spiritual-cum-militant fraternity, which shaped the future history of North-West India. The personal Guruship also ended with Guru Gobind Singh and the spiritual authority was vested in the Sikh scripture, *Guru Granth Sahib*.

Guru Nanak and his successors saw the conflict of two religious cultures, Hinduism, the polytheistic faith on one side and Islam, the monotheistic religion on the other. The Hindu was the idol-worshipper and the Muslim was the idol-breaker. The Hindu society was a caste-ridden society. With the lapse of time, the mutual intercourse led to mutual understanding. The Hindu conception of caste-system developed gradually among the Muslims. "Mutual contact developed new castes

49

and sub-castes. Various classes of Muslims began to reside separately in different localities even in the some town, for example Sheikhs and Sayyids. The lower functional groups were organised on the model of the Hindu caste-system with their Panchayats or caste councils and officers to enforce the observance of caste rules by the time-honoured sanction of boy-cotting. Mutual jealousies among the foreign and Indian Muslim nobles and Amirs of the Sultan developed caste-like groups in the higher and aristocratic Muslim society. The conception of untouchability evolved in due course in the Muslim society. The lower caste persons of the Hindu society were converted to Islam in large numbers due to tyranny of caste-system, the prospects of escape from the poll-tax and other social advantages. These new converts were treated like untouchables in the Muslim society. They were given neither any share in the administration nor any place in the Muslim aristocracy. They were neither treated on a footing of equality with other Muslims nor could enjoy power with higher Muslims."[1] Such caste-distinctions and their resultant injustice to various sections of society were decried by the Sikh Gurus and the saint-poets of Guru Granth Sahib. They envisaged a casteless and classless society. They proclaimed equality for all. For them the whole humanity was like one family, irrespective of caste, creed and colour. They preached the brotherhood of man.

> The whole humanity is under one shade
> Therefore all the caste and name distinctions
>       be damned.
>             (Sri Raga Ki Var, Shlok M. I).

> Do not be proud of your caste
> He is virtually a Brahmin, who realises Brahman
> Do not be proud of your caste, O fool,
> Several evils proceed from this pride.
>             (Bhairo, M.III)

> If though art a Brahmin, born of Brahmin woman,
> Then why hast thou not come through another path?
> Since when art thou a Brahmin and I a Shudra?

Since when I am blood and thou art milk?
                    (Gauri Kabir)


Some one is Hindu, some one Turk,
Some one is Rafzi, Some one Imam Shafi,
Consider all the humanity as one and the same.
                    (Akal Ustat, M. X)


Their eyes are similar, ears similar, bodies
                    similar and habits are similar.
All human being are amalgam of earth, air, fire and water.
                    (Akal Ustat, M. X)


There has always been division of society into various classes, the basis being either religious, economic or political. The populace has either been exploited by the priestly class, or by bourgeoise or by the king and his ministers. All such exploitation has been denounced in Sikhism. The Pandit and Brahmin of Hinduism and the Mullah and Qadi of Islam sacrificed truth and justice for their personal ends. The affluent and lowly received different treatment at their hands.

Kabir addressed the Pandit in the following manner:-


O Pundit! What ill-advice thou hast adopted?
Thou wilt be drowned alongwith thy family
Why dost thou not remember the Lord, O unfortunate
                    one!
What is the use of studying Vedas and Puranas like
                    an ass's burden of sandalwood?
Thou dost not understand the value of the Name of
                    the Lord.
Thou dost declare the bondage of the spirit as *Dharma*
Then whom wilt thou call *adharma* ?
Thou dost establish thyself as a sage,
Then whom should we call a butcher?
Thou dost not know thyself, thy mind is blind
Why dost thou instruct others?

51

Thou dost sell learning for *maya*,
Thy life will pass away uselessly
                    (Maru Kabir, p.1102-03)

Guru Nanak Dev said:

The Pundit studies scriptures, but does not
                    understand the crux,
He instructs others and trades in *maya*.
                    (Sri M. 1., p.56)

Guru Nanak Dev talked openly of the exploitation by the *Qadi*, Brahmin
and Yogi:-

Qadi tells lies and accepts bribe
Brahmin takes a bath but kills jivas
Yogi is blind and does not know the path
All the three lead towards destruction.
                    (Dhanasari, M.I, p.662)

The king acted like a lion and fed on the flesh and blood of his
subjects. His ministers and other officers acted like dogs.

Guru Nanak Dev said:

The kings are lions and the officers are dogs
Who disturb the subjects at odd hours.
Their servants injure them (the subjects) with
                    their claws,
And cause the dogs to drink their blood.
                    (Var Malar, M.1 p.1288)

Such kings and their officers, who do not care for their subjects and
indulge in all sorts of vices are the cause of revolutions. When Babur
invaded India, Guru Nanak saw with his own eyes the pitiable plight of
not only the people, but also of the erstwhile rulers. He has depicted his

experiences in a few exquisite hymns.

He said:

> The kings have lost balance by merry-making
> The terror of Babur spread everywhere
> And the prince could not get food to eat.
>
> (Asa M.1, p.417)

The Guru concluded that the reign of that king becomes steady, who follows the democratic ideals.[2]

Undoubtedly, in the recent past, Karl Marx wrote "Freeman and slave, patrician and plebeion, Lord and serf, guildmaster and journeyman, in a word, oppressor and oppressed, stood in constant opposition to one another, carried on uninterrupted, now hidden, now open fight, a fight that each time ended, either in a revolutionary reconstitution of society at large, or in the common ruin of the contending classes," but it was Guru Nanak, who, five centuries earlier, openly spoke of the exploiter and the exploited, the oppressor and the oppressed. He also talked of revolution in society and the democratic ideals.

The Sikh Gurus denounced all formalism and symbolism, all rites and sacraments, all prejudices and barriers. Their religion is based on three main tenets:—

1. Remembrance of the Name of the Lord,
2. Doing work and
3. Sharing the earnings with the needy.

The first tenet is missing from the ideology of Karl Marx. For him the religion is the opium of the masses: man makes religion, not religion makes man. According to him, "It is precisely because he no longer feels at home in this world that man takes refuge in another world which is above and outside reality. Religion is not the cause but the result of man's alienation." For him the material world is the only reality and the economic principle, the fundamental principle to all phenomena in the society. For Sikh Gurus, such a concept is merely one-sided. The world is an amalgam of matter and spirit. Both are inter-connected, therefore for a fuller view of reality, we have to build up a relation with our source, the

Real Reality. The conception of Marx that religion is the opium of the masses has no validity for Sikh Religion, because Sikhism never takes a disciple above and outside reality. Every individual is required to work. The religion of Guru Nanak is a religion of house-holders and workers. It emphatically denounces asceticism and monasticism:

"Do all the work with hand and feet and keep the
mind attuned with the Lord"
(Shalok Kabir, p.1376)

In Marx, action was given specificity in a radical emphasis on *work*. "Man becomes alive through work, for through work man loses his isolation and becomes a social or co-operative being, and thus learns of himself: and through work he is able to transform nature as well."

The Marxian doctrine of work was forestalled by the Sikh Gurus and the saint poets of *Guru Granth Sahib*. The Gurus not only laid emphasis on work, but also initiated the institution of *Langar* or free kitchen. In the house of Guru Nanak at Kartarpur, every visitor had an access to the kitchen. Balwand, the musician at the court of the second Guru, has talked about the free kitchen of the second Guru:

Mother Khivi (the wife of Guru Angad) is a
noble person and is like a tree of dense shade.
In her free kitchen, wealth is distributed.
There is Khir mixed with ghee which tasted like nectar.
(Var Satta Balwand, Ramkali, p.967)

Guru Amar Das, the Third Guru refused to meet a visitor, if he had not sat with other common-folk in the *langar* and taken food in the common kitchen. This rule was even not relaxed in the case of Akbar, the King Emperor.

This institution of free kitchen has continued since the days of Guru Nanak. Any person with any creed, caste or colour can partake food in the *langar*. The lowliest of man sits with the highest dignitaries in this kitchen. One becomes ego-less and conscious of equality of all human beings. This is socialism in practice, but this is not enough. Every Sikh is enjoined to share his earnings with the needy. The weaker sections of

54

the society must be helped to rise in status. This is the philosophy of *take (daswand)*, which is meant to raise the economic status of common people by creating avenues for employment in different trades and industries. The Khalsa is expected to accumulate wealth and institute free kitchens and stores which are to provide food to the hungry, clothes to the naked and fulfil the requirements of the needy.[4] There is a great responsibility of the State in this direction. It should look after the needs of the subjects regarding food, shelter and clothing. A hungry person can only think of filling his belly.[5] Kabir addresses the Lord in the following manner:-

"There can be no devotion, when hunger afflicts
Take away thy rosary, (O Lord)"[6]

All the troubles crop up when the masses face oppression and discrimination. They are exploited by the upper classes, jeopardising their freedom. There is anguish because of class-conflict. The exploitation of man by man can only end by the order of the Graceful Lord. Guru Arjan Dev says:-

The Graceful Lord has now ordered
Therefore none is exploited
All live in peace and comfort
And there is sovereignty of modesty.[7]

Therefore a State without exploitation can become a reality only by the will of the Lord. According to Marx the freedom of man consists in bringing all those external factors under control which are responsible for the unfreedom of man. Most important factors for unfreedom are private property and division of labour. The private property creates individualism what is responsible for the emergence of the class of workers and of the capitalists. The harmful sting of individualism can be made ineffective by doing away with the ego by the Grace of the Lord.

The Sovereignty of modesty is the resultant. The ego can be subdued in the company or society of good people, where one learns the practice of virtues in life. Hedonism and asceticism are decried and emphasis is laid on social service and *Nishkama Karma*.

According to Marx, by doing away with all classes, we can establish a classless society i.e. communism, in which the following formula will be realised:

"From each according to his abilities and to each according to his needs."

In this society every person will be an object of appropriation to every other man. One will be free to do whatever he is capable of. Can such a society become a reality or it will remain a dream for ever? In Hindu mythology the age in which such a society will emerge is known as *Satyuga* (the age of truth). Plato in his great dialogues of "Republic" has discussed the nature of an ideal city State. He says in Book Fourth, "We founded our city so as to be at its very best, as well as we could, since we know well that in the good city surely Justice would be. What we found there then, let us apply to the single man, and if it be found to agree, well and good, but if something else becomes manifest in the one man, we will come back to the city and test it. So by examining them side by side and rubbing them together like fire-sticks, we may very likely make justice flash out, and when it shows itself, we may confirm it for ourselves." There is no surety if such a city state would ever became a reality, but Ravidas, a great saint, has actually visited such a city state in a moment of spiritual ecstasy. He says:

Begampura (abode of bliss) is the name of the city
There is neither grief nor anxiety
There is neither trouble nor any tax on commodities,
No fear, no blemish, no downfall.
Now I have achieved entry in this good land
Where there is always peace
Where rule is steadfast and eternal
None is of second or third state, all are equal.
The fame of this habitation is eternal
Where every one is affluent and contented.
The residents move freely according to their will
They are acquainted with the abode and no one stands in their way.
Ravidas, the cobbler, enjoys freedom and says

Whosoever is the fellow citizen, he is my friend.

(Gauri Guareri Ravidas—p.345)

Such an ideal state can become a reality, if every one takes refuge in the Lord and adopts the high ethical qualities.

Equality of human beings on the basis of sex is also emphasised in Sikhism. In medieval age the woman was in pitiable plight, not only in India, but also in other countries. She was considered much inferior to man and was merely a means of pleasure and procreation for man. Undoubtedly, woman was held in high veneration in the Vedic age. Tantras also considered her to be the embodiment on earth of the supreme Shakti Who Pervades the universe. But her status in society was significantly reduced in middle ages, when in India, she was known as the "Shoe of the Foot". The Yogis abhorred her, the priests exploited her. Manu had given her a menial position in Hindu society. She was considered an obstacle in the way of spiritual progress. But the Sikh Gurus were critical of all such opposition for womanhood. Guru Nanak Dev said:

We are born of women, we are borne by women,
We are married to women, we develop friendship with women
All the system flourishes through the women,
When dead, we search for another woman,
All the relationships are through women.
Why to talk ill of her who gives birth to the kings.
A woman gives birth to a woman,
Besides a woman, there is only One True Lord.

(Var Asa, M.I)

The custom of *Sati* prevalent in Hindu society was decried by Guru Amar Das. He said:

Those women cannot be called *Satis*, who burn
themselves on the funeral pyres with their husbands,
They are *Satis* only who die of the shock of separation
They may also be considered *Satis*, who are embodiment
Of character and contentment.

57

Who serve their Lords and always remember them.
(Var Suhi, Slok M. III)

Bhai Gurdas, the great Sikh theologian says:˙

She is better-half and the door of salvation
The woman is a fruit of peace for *Gurmukh*.

The Metaphor of wife and husband pervades the bani of *Guru Granth Sahib*. This shows the profound veneration of the Sikh Gurus for 'woman'. The woman is to be given due freedom for education, worship, work etc. The sons and daughters are the creation of the Lord, therefore they should be treated on equal footing. 'One man and one woman' this is the motto regarding the nuptial bond in Sikhism. It is the golden rule.˙ The family life can remain peaceful and happy if husband and wife both remain faithful to each other. The tussle will begin if any one swerves from this ideal.

In Hindu society the birth of a girl in a family was considered inauspicious which resulted in the heinous crime of infanticide. Out of the fear of lustful Muslim chiefs, the *Parda System* (seclusion of woman) and child marriage came into vogue. The woman depended on her husband or his relatives and was not allowed to participate in all the social functions, rites and ceremonies. In order to protect her honour the customs of *Jauhar* and *Sati* were prevalent. All this was rejected by the Sikh Gurus who brought in a reformation of society.

In Muslim society slavery was common and this unhealthy feature also crept in the social life of the Hindu society. But such an exploitation of man by man could never be accepted by Guru Nanak. He, in fact, was a friend of the lowliest in society˙ and wanted to raise their status.

As a result of the contact of the Muslim culture, the Hindus adopted the Muslim dress and ceremonial. They also began to talk in the languages spoken by Muslims. Such slavish mentality war decried by the Guru, who said;

1.  Atharva has become the Veda of the iron age (Kaliyuga) and the name of God is Allah The Blue dress has been adopted and the

Muslim ceremonial is being imitated.

(Var Asa, M-1)

2.    . . . The Lord now seems to be in blue dress in every home, the word *Mian* is muttered And you have adopted a foreign language.

(Bssant Hindol, M.I, Page 119)

The Guru was very sore regarding the adoption of an outsider's dress and language. This meant desertion of one's own culture and losing one's independent entity.

The vices of gambling and wine drinking, which were common in Muslim society, penetrated into Hindu society. Such vices made the society immoral. With the rise in moral stature, a society becomes great. The cardinal virtues must be adopted by all the members of a society. This is the real *Dharma*. In Sikhism emphasis is laid on *Dharma*, the path of piety and righteousness.

Guru Nanak Says:

"The thieves, sex maniacs and gamblers will be crushed like sesame."

(Var Malar, M. 1)

Bhai Gurudas writs;

Those who drink, gamble and rape other's wives,
Those who are unfaithful and ungrateful are the sinners and killers.

(Var 34)

Regarding wine-drinking it is recorded in Guru Granth Sahib

1.   By drinking which one loses wisdom, becomes mad, loses power of discrimination and is kicked out by the Lord
By drinking which the Lord is forgotten and one is punished in the court of the Lord
Such a false wine should not be taken as far as possible.

(Var Bihagra) Shlok M. 3. p. 554

2.    By drinking this wine Saith Nanak, one earns many vices (Var
Bihagra Shlok M.3, p.553)

Thus in order to save one's self from such vices, he is enjoined to
follow the path of Dharma.

Guru Arjan says:-

Do not delay in the acts of Dharma
But cause delay in sinful acts
                 (Shlok Sahaskriti)

Every culture regards some virtues as primary. They are called
cardinal virtues. Greek culture regarded wisdom, courage, temperance
and justice as cardinal virtues. In Christianity, three more i.e. faith, hope
and love were added. In Hinduism, Jainism and Buddhism stress has been
laid on *Ahimsa* and tolerance. But in Sikhism the godly qualities, which
are practicable in the life of a disciple, are the cardinal virtues. Since the
ultimate goal of a Sikh is the union with the Lord, he is instructed to
imbibe the qualities through which he can inhale the Divinity within his
self. God is Truth, Just, Sweet of speech, Love, Fearless etc. etc.
Therefore a Sikh should imbibe such qualities in order to attain nearness
to the Lord. Two attributes of God mentioned in the *Mul Mantra* (or the
primary formula of the Sikhs) i.e. *Nirbhau* (devoid of fear) and Nirvair
(Devoid of enmity) are the cardinal virtues practised by the Khalsa and
these are the basis of the golden history of the Sikhs.

A Sikh lives two lives at the same time, the mundane and the
spiritual. He earns to live and live for God realization. He combines
within himself the wordliness and saintliness. On one band, he is a man
of the world, working hard for the welfare of family, the society and the
State and on the other hand he rises above mere worldliness, living the life
of a saint. He is like a lotus born and bred in water but rising above the
surface of water. As a man of the world, he is a fruitful partner, loving
parent, truthful dealer and a sincere worker. Though outwardly attached
with all his dealings and duties, he is inwardly working for his ultimate
goal. He attends to his normal work as well as the holy congregation. The
swords of *miri* (worldy grandeur) and *Piri* (spiritual greatness) worn by

the sixth Guru are his ideal. He is a *Raja Yogi* in this sense. He lives a full life, activating both the body and the soul.

Sikhism is a monotheistic faith. It believes in both the aspects of Brahman, the Transcendent as well as Immanent, but adores only the former, which is beyond the fold of maya. Therefore it rejects all the gods, spirits and incarnations, who take birth and perish away. They are not immortal. In this respect, Sikhism stands apart from most of the religions, God in Sikhism is without any form, colour and delineation, therefore the idol-worship or image—worship has no place in Sikhism;

"Why to adore the other one, who takes birth and dies down?"
(Var Gujri M.3, p.509)

The Sikh temples have no idols and images, Their scripture, Guru Grnath Sahib, is thier preceptor, the object of highest veneration, which gives knowledge of the Absolute. The hymns contained in the scripture, are recited and sung by the individuals and congregations. There is no priestly class in Sikhism. There is a keeper-cum-thaologian in every Sikh temple, who is required to be well-versed in Sikh scripture. He recites the verses from the Scripture. The musicians sing the hymns in praise of the Lord in the congregation in the presence of Guru Granth Sahib. The Musicians and the keeper need not be professional.

No formal practices are joined for the Sikhs. Guru Nanak has rejected all *Karma Kanda* and *Upasana Kanda*. The emphasis is on *Gyan Kanda* i.e. the attainment of knowledge. The knowledge comes from the Guru. Through the absorption in the verses of *Guru Granth Sahib*, the Sikh gets knowledge and guidance. The Saints and *Brahm Gianis* (the knowers of Brahman), who have already traversed the path, assist him in his endeavours. The Sikh being a man of action, is a *Karma Yogi*, being a devotee of the Lord, is a *Bhakta Yogi* and being a man of knowledge, is *Gyan Yogi*. In fact, he is an amalgam of *Karma Yoga, Bhakti Yoga* and *Gyan Yoga*. In other words he is a soldier, saint and scholar at the same time. Such a 'model man' is not found anywhere else other than Sikh Culture.

The ultimate goal in Sikhism is the union with the Lord. But this union or Yoga is very much different from *Tantra Yoga, Kundalini Yoga*

61

or *Hath Yoga* involving pranas and nerves. This yoga is known as *Nam yoga* or *Surt-shabad yoga*. It requires no special *asanas* (Postures). It is also called *Sahaj Yoga*, because the devotee rises above the three states known as Jagrit (awakening), *Svapana* (dream) and *Sushupti* (dreamless sleep). He absorbs himself completely in the Name of the Lord. The repetition of the Name becomes spontaneous. Every breath and every pore of the body is saturated with the Name of the Lord. Through this facile process, the real objective of life is realised. Such a process is within the reach of every individual and this is the best method for the attainment of the supreme state i.e. *Sahaj* or *Turiya*. The Guru (or preceptor) is a 'must' for the spiritual guidance and this Guruship is not 'personal', it is the "Word" that works wonders for the realization of the "Wonderful Lord".

No special time or period is fixed for the practice of *Sahaj yoga* or *Bhakti yoga*. The Lord can be remembered at all times and in all the stages of life by all men, irrespective of their status in society. The Sikh Gurus rejected *varnas* and *ashrams* both. Out of the four stages of life mentioned in Hinduism, the second stage i.e. *Grahasthya Ashramas* has been considered best in Sikhism, because it is the stage of activity, which should continue throughout life. If every one in the society works according to his/her position and status, several evils can be avoided. There will be no beggary, no wastage of time and energy, no brawls, no fanaticism and instead there will be healthy and constructive atmosphere.

The religious culture of the Sikhs has made a significant contribution in giving a lead to the humanity regarding the lesson of "high spirits" (*charhdi Kala*) in every eventuality. This makes a disciple stable and steadfast. He recites "Anand" (the third Guru's hymn on Bliss) in all the events of both happiness and sorrow. This quality make him the embodiment of courage and fearlessness. He neither fears nor frightens. He rises above duality, always living in the presence of One-the Absolute Lord. He is a warrior/soldier in the battlefield of life.

Sikh religion is universal and practical. The high and low, male and female, rich and poor—every one can practise it, because it is without any formal practices, rites and ceremonies. The Guru wanted his Sikhs to live high on moral and spiritual planes. He said once "I Shall take the Panth to higher planes"

For this purpose he ordained a discipline for his disciples. This world is a training ground, where the Sikh receives the necessary practical education. The objective of education, according to Sikh Gurus, is to raise the moral and spiritual standard of the human beings. It ought to make one philanthropic.

The Sikh Gurus preached their gospel in the language of th masses. No special language may be called divine. The Lord talks to us in our tongue, which can enter into the inner recesses of our heart. The Word of God comes through the Word of Guru. We can be attuned with the Lord through this Word or *Akshara*.

The bani of *Guru Granth Sahib* is musical and metrical. Music plays a great part in the realisation of the ecstatic state or Sahaj. Music is a beneficial remedy for physical and mental ailments also. Plato believed in it. The Sikh Gurus think likewise, but also consider it as food for divine love. Several schools of music flourished in India before the birth of Sikhism; the professional musicians were employed in the temples, but the Gurus brought it to the common man. Guru Arjan Dev says;

He who listens to the kirtan (divine Music) of Hari and also sings it,
He does not suffer any ailment.
(Gauri M.5, p. 190)

The Muslims have been averse to music, but they have been great promoters of architecture. They built very beautiful mosques, forts and mausoleums. Sikhism has brought a unique innovation in the creation of its temples. Since the Lord is All-Pervading, the Sikh temples have the entrance in all the four directions.

The Sikh religious culture has the whole humanity in view for the spiritual amelioration. Guru Amar Das says "The World is burning, Protect it by Thy Grace, O Lord, Give it emancipation by any means." (Var Bilaval, p. 853) The spiritual ascent, has been described by Guru Nanak in his master-piece 'Japuji'. From the region of *Dharma* one rises through the help of the Guru to the region of Knowledge. From thence he proceeds to the region of effort, where his mind and intellect are purified. Then he enters the region of Grace, from where the Graceful Lord takes him to His region of Truth. The Guru is helpful all along the path. Following the path of Dharma one gains knowledge and strength for effort. Then with the Grace of the Lord he attains the final beatitude.

This is, in, nutshell, the contribution of the Sikh religious culture towards human uplift.

## REFERENCES

1. Evolution of Indian Culture by B.N. Luniya, IIIed, p.428
2. Maru M.1, p. 992
3. Daniel Bell: "The Debate on Alienation" in Revisionism: Essays on the History of Marxist Ideas: ed. Leopold Labedz: (London: Allen and Unwin, 1962) p. 199
4. Karni Nama.
5. Gauri Guareri M. 4, p. 164
6. Sorath Kabir Page—656
7. Sri Raaga M. 5, p.74
8. Eka Nari Jati Hoe, (Bhai Gurdas)
9. Sri Raga M. 1, p. 15.

# The All-Ebmracing Sikh Scripture

The great scripture of Sikhism "Guru Granth Sahib" is a unique gift for the whole world. Its subject is the Universal Father "Para Brahman" and "Param-Ishvara" and also the human being of the whole universe. It encloses the whole world in its fold, where the children of the same Father live. Under the influence of different geographical conditions and climates, the human beings of various colours are the Creation of the same Universal Father. This fact has been expressed by Guru Arjan Dev in the following way:

Thou art the Universal Lord, Our Father,
Thy nine treasures are Thy Stores, always full,
Whomsoever Thou Bestowest, he gets full satisfaction;
And he is Thy True devotee.
Everyone has taken refuge in Thee,
And Thou art present in every heart,
None considers Thee as an outsider.
Thou Bestowest salvation Thyself on the Enlightened one
Thou Thyself Makest the self-willed ones transmigrate
I am a sacrifice to Thee,
All is Thy Sport and Show.

(Majh M.5, p.97).

Kabir has also said:

I am Thy son and Thou art my Father;
We abide in the same place.

(Asa Kabir, p.476).

He calls His father as "The Great Master of the Universe," Whom every son is duty-bound to realise:

My Father is the Great Master of the Universe,
How should I go to That Father?
The True Guru shows the Path, when we meet him;
My mind is absorbed in the Father of the universe.
(Asa Kabir, p.476)

It is only the True Guru, who takes us to the Universal Father, Who has the whole world in His Sight and Who wants to emancipate all the Jivas:

The True Guru is such, as wants the salvation of all.
(Sri Rag M.1, p.72).

The True Guru wants the good of all.
(Var Gauri M.4, p.312).

Even a calumniator who comes under the refuge of the True Guru,
The True Guru forgives him for the past sins and unites him with the
holy congregation,
Just as during rain, the water of streets, streams and ponds mixes
with the water of the Ganges and becomes pure.
Such is the merit of the non-inimical True Guru that whosoever
meets him, is absolved of hunger and thirst and attains
peace;
Look at this wonder of the True king; whosoever bows before the
True Guru, he is loved by everybody.
(Var Bilawal M.4, pp.854-55).

But this is the desire of the True Guru that the human being should be emancipated, though it may be through any Path. Guru Amar Das says:

O Lord, the world is burning, kindly save it through Your Grace,
Emancipate it through any Path Approved by You.
(Var Bilawal M.4, Shalok M.3, p.853).

There are several spiritual disciplines in the world, which have their own founders. Talking about the six systems of Hindu philosophy, Guru Nanak Dev has said:

> There are six Shastras, their six Gurus and the six instructions;
> But the Guru of these Gurus is One, who has adopted several guises.
> It will be your merit to accept that discipline,
> Which sings the Praises of the Lord.
> The Sun is one but seasons (Produced by the Sun) are many
> The Lord has put on several garbs.
> (Asa M.1, p.12)

In this quotation, the Guru has mentioned the six Shastras (Samkhya, Yoga, Vaisheshika, Nyaya, Purva-Mimamsa and Uttara Mimamsa) of the six preceptors (Kapila, Patanjali, Kannada, Gautama, Jaimini and Vyasa). The Guru of these Gurus is the Lord Himself. According to Guru Nanak Dev, the human being should accept only that discipline, which sings the Praises of the Lord.

Talking about the Muslims, the Guru says:

> "It is difficult to be called a Muslim. If he has these qualities, then he is one. First let the Faith of Allah be sweet to him, then let him scrub his ego and with faith in the Prophet, let him submit to the Will of Allah . . . and be merciful to all creatures; then he is acclaimed as a true Muslim" (Var Majh M. 1, p.141).

In this Shloka, the Guru has accepted only that person a Muslim, who scrubs his ego and vices and remain in the discipline of the Prophet. He should resign himself to the Will to the Lord and be merciful to all.

Guru Arjan Dev, differentiating between this world and the next, has said that whosoever wants to refrain another person from the spiritual side and gets him absorbed in the world, is a criminal. He considers both the aspects essential. He says:

> He who causes one to leave the spiritual side and absorb himself solely in the world, he is called a criminal in both the worlds. The true religion puts us on path of virtue and goodness, but leaning on

67

the the side of religion, we should not overlook the worldly aspect. Only the One Lord awakes within all and directs them on their paths. (Suhi M.5, p.742-43).

In this way, *Guru Granth Sahib* manifests a very liberal viewpoint, according to which every human being, being the son of the same spiritual Father, deserves unity with Him. In whichever religious brotherhood he has taken birth, he should practise its discipline closely.

The instruction of *Guru Granth Sahib* is not meant for any specific nation, sect, caste or brotherhood, it is common for all humanity. In the house of the Lord, no special significance is attached to any specific caste or brotherhood; there is no differentiation there between a Brahmin and a Shudra. Only the actions of a person are considered there. Guru Nanak Dev says:

It may be told that in the True House there is no consideration of caste and birth. whatever actions one performs, they only make his caste and birth. (Prabhati M.1, p.1330).

This is the reason why Guru Arjan Dev has written very clearly:

The instruction is common for all the four castes: Brahmin, Kshatriya, Vaishya and Shudra. He who remembers the Name of the Lord is emancipated in the Iron age . . . (Suhi M.5, pp.747-48).

Kshatriya, Brahmin, Shudra and Vaishya—all are emancipated by the same Name of the Lord. He who listens to the instruction attains salvation. (Maru M.5, p.1001).

Undoubtedly, the *dvijas* (Brahmins, Kshatriyas and Vaishyas), after wearing the thread, had been considered worthy of leading a spiritual life, but Guru Nanak Dev did not consider the sacred thread of any use because it was destructible. The real sacred thread is the spiritual thread, which contains the cotton of mercy, the thread of contentment, the knots of continence and the twists of truth. This sacred thread is imperishable. The Guru Says:

68

The cotton of mercy, the thread of contentment, the knots of continence and the twist of truth, if you have this sacred thread of the soul, then put it on me, O Pundit! It does not break and does not get dirty. It does not burn or perish. Blessed are those men who put such thread around their necks. It is bought for four *kauris* and worn on the sacred platform, the instruction is given in the ear and the Brahmin becomes the Guru. When the man dies, the thread is burnt and the soul goes in the next world without the thread. (Var Asa M.1, p.471).

According to the Guru, the Shudras and menial castes, who have become a prey to the human prejudices and untouchability, deserve much greater sympathy. He says:

The lowest of the lowest castes and the lowest of all;
The Lord is on their side, then why to imitate the high-ups?
Wherever the lowly are protected, there is Your Grace, O Lord!
(Sri Rag, M.1, p.15).

Guru Nanak Dev, the Guru of the world met various types of *fakirs, darveshes,* saints and Sadhus in India and abroad during his four journeys; he met householders, workers, Buddhists, Jainas, Sufis, Yogis, Pundits, teachers, Mullahs, Thugs, thiefs, heretics, demons, Vaishanavas, Shaivas, Shaktas etc.—various types and categories of people. He found that person nowhere whom he sought. He had seen at several places violence and bloodshed. The people had called him a "Kurahia" (One who has been misled). Several Momins had tried to stone him to death at Mecca. He held discussions with contemporary religious leaders and conveyed to them his concept of real Religion. He had given his views about Vedas, Katebs (the Semitic religious texts), Shastras and smritis. Before going on his missionary journey he had cast his inner sight on the whole world. Bhai Gurdas says in this connection:

The Baba saw the world to its extreme limits. (Var I)
Baba saw with concentration the whole world burning. (Var I).

In order to give the right direction to the burning world, the Guru met all types of people, whether they were kings or poor subjects, whether they were saints or thieves. He himself has written:

I have set out on my Journeys in order to search for a *Gurmukh* (an enlightened person). (Siddh Goshta, p.939).

According to him, the world was created for the *Gurmukh*. In the world full of ego, the *Dharma* had disappeared. Such a state of the world has been depicted by the Guru in the following way:

The *Kaliyuga* (Iron age) is the knife and the kings are butchers, the *Dharma* has flown away. The dark night of falsehood has spread and the moon of truth is not seen rising (in the sky). I have searched but have not found the path in darkness. I am weeping, having been engrossed in ego. How can I get release? (Var Majh M.1, p.145).

The Guru was against the walls of prejudices created between man and man. When the same Reality is pervading the whole universe, then why there are prejudices and divisions everywhere? Why a man should hate a man? Why should there be the class-division of Brahmin, Kshatriya, Vaishya and Shudra? Why should a Brahmin consider a Shudra untouchable? Why a king should suppress his subjects? Why one person should live a life of luxury and the other a life of poverty? Why all the people should not work? why the persons who do not work, be given respect? Why every person should not perform his work and duties properly?
He said:

1. He is only a Brahmin, who realises Brahman. (Shalok, p.1411)
2. He is a Kshatriya, who is a warrior of actions. (Shalok, p.1411).
3. He is an Udasi, who observes detachment. (Var Ramkali, p.952).
4. He is a true king, whose treasure is the Name. (Dakhni Oamkar, p.930).
5. He is a Sannyasi . . . who destroys his ego. (Maru, p.1013).
6. He is a Giani, who is in tune with the Word. (Bilawal, p.831).
7. He is a Yogi, who knows the discipline. (Dhanasari, p.662).
8. He is a Muslim, who washes away his dirt. (Dhanasari, p.662). etc. etc.

70

The Guru, compiled the compositions of earlier radical saints in his *Pothi*, whose thoughts were identical with his thoughts. Later on Guru Amar Das and Guru Arjan Dev gathered together the compositions of the saints and the Gurus. In A.D. 1604, the *Granth Sahib* was ready. The compiler of this recension, known as *Kartarpuri Bir*, was Guru Arjan Dev and the scribe was Bhai Gurdas. Later on in *Damdame wali Bir* (the recension prepared at Damdama Sahib by Guru Gobind Singh, with Bhai Mani Singh as scribe), the compositions of the ninth Guru, Guru Tegh Bahadur were added. The first recension was installed in *Hari Mandir* (The Golden Temple) by the fifth Guru, Guru Arjan Dev and when the last Guru, Guru Gobind Singh was on the verge of possing away, he bestowed the Guruship on *Damdame wali Bir* or the Adi Granth, thereby ending the lines of personal Guruship and also bequeathing to posterity a sacred treasure for the salvation of humanity.

*Guru Granth Sahib* (also called the *Adi Granth* in order to differentiate it from *Dasam Granth,* (the Book of the Tenth Guru) can, indeed, be called a Parliament of saints. In this Parliamentst, the saint Jaidev of Bengal, belonging to twelfth Century, the Sufi saint sheikh Baba Farid, belonging to twelfth-thirteenth century, the saints Namdev and Trilochan of Maharashtra, belonging to the fourteenth century, the famous saints of Uttar Pradesh including Ramanand, Kabir, Ravidas, Pipa and Sain, belonging to fifteenth century. Alongwith Guru Nanak Dev, Guru Angad Dev, Guru Amar Das, Guru Ram Das, Guru Arjan Dev and Guru Tegh Bahadur, also sit the saint Beni, Saint Sadhna of Sind, Saint Parmanand of Barsi (Sholapur), Saint Dhanna of Deoli, Rajputana, Sufi Saint Bhikhan of Kakori, Lucknow, saint Sur Das, the governor of Sandilya, In this Parliament the Brahmin, Kshatriya, Vaishya, Shudra and Sufi all have their seats together.

The Sikh Gurus and the Saints, who though represent various parts of India and lived from the twelfth to the seventeenth century—their compositions are not meant for the people of one state, country or region; they are for the whole world and for all times. They are all the great men of all the humanity and they have produced a common treasure, which is for every nation, every tribe, every class, every caste and every country. The people are now awakening to this fact. The comments of some great scholars are given hereunder:

Dr. Radhakrishnan, the great philosopher and erstwhile President of

71

India says:

> Nanak Dev affirms the possibility of holy life in all religions. the philosophy of ecumenism which is now becoming popular, was anticipated by the Sikh Gurus. No wonder that the *Adi Granth,* which is the sacred scripture of the Sikhs, contains the utterances of the holy men of both Hinduism and Islam....*Adi Granth* establishes a real dialogue at the level of religions. This dialogue never degenerates into a dispute in the *Adi Granth.* . . . The Sikh Gurus regarded Themselves as human and not divine...The barriers which the Sikh Gurus sought to cast down are again being built. Many pernicious practices are creeping into our lives. (from "Guru Nanak—His Life,Time and Teachings")

Dr. Suniti Kumar Chatterji, the great linguist and scholar of India, writes:

> Three great things are to be noted in the social ideology of Guru Nanak. One was the entire abandonment of the caste idea. . . . The second great thing to be noticed in Guru Nanak Deva's social views was that he did not countenance enforced celibacy as a vital necessity for spiritual endeavour and spiritual attainment. . . . The third matter which at once distinguishes Guru Nanak from the average run of religious men and women was his great love of man as man and his sense of equality of the entire human race, (from "Guru Nanak—A Heritage")

Mrs. Pearl S. Buck, the Nobel Laureate writes:

> Shri Guru Granth Sahib is a source-book, an expression of man's loneliness, his aspirations, his longings, his cry to God and his hunger for communication with that Being. I have studied the scriptures of other great religions, but I do not find elsewhere the same power of appeal to the heart and mind as I find here in these volumes. They are compact inspite of their length and are a revelation of the vast reach of the human heart, varying from the most noble concept of God, to the recognition and indeed the insistence upon the practical needs of the human body. There is

something strangely modern about these scriptures and this puzzled me until I learned that they are in fact comparatively modern, compiled as late as the sixteenth century, when explorers were beginning to discover that the globe in which we all live is a single entity divided only by arbitrary line, of our own making. . . . Perhaps this sense of unity is the source of power I find in these volumes. they speak to persons of any religion or of none They speak for the human heart and the searching mind...One wonders what might have been produced if the founders of the Sikh religion had been acquainted with the findings of modern science. where would their quest for knowledge have led them had science been their means instead of religion? Perhaps in the same direction, for the most important revelation now being made by scientists is that their knowledge, as it opens one door after another to the many universes in external existence, affirms the essential unity of science and religion. It is impressive and significant that in the study of these Sikh scriptures we see the affirmation through the approach of the brilliant minds and deep searching hearts of men who are part of India. Through them we see a Beyond that belongs to us all. The result is a universal revelation". (from the first volume of the Translation of "Sri Guru Granth Sahib" by Dr. Gopal Singh).

Thus *Guru Granth Sahib* is an All-Embracing scripture. It contains such *bani* as in the words of Professor Puran Singh "is the godly companion of the soul after death and helps it and also resounds as divine music in the invisible regions". This *bani* is saturated with divine ambrosia and when it goes deep down in the heart, all the sorrows and troubles end (Sorath M.5, p.628). The singing of this *bani* ever brings peace and comfort (Sorath M.5, p.629). This *bani* resides in the heart with the Grace of the Lord. It is the light of the world (Sri Rag M.3, p.67). The knowledge of the Name of the Lord comes from this *bani*, which unites us with the Lord (Maru M.3, p.1066). This *bani* is the store-house of devotion. Those who sing or listen to it and practise its istruction, they are blessed by the Lord (Asa M.5, p.376). This *bani* which unites with the Universal Father is perennial like the Immortal Father. It becomes the prop of a true Sikh (Suhi M.4, p.759). This *bani* of the Guru, having the spirit of the Guru in it, is also called the Guru (Nat M.4, p.982). Blessed is that True Guru, who has given instructions through this *bani* for the welfare of humanity:

> That True Guru, the Perfect one be blessed and glorified,
> Who, giving his injunctions regarding the Lord Has reformed the
> Whole world.
>
> (Var Vadhans M.4, p.586).

# Sikh Martyrs

*The Concept of a Martyr in Sikhism*

The word prevalent for 'martyr' in India is *Shahid,* which connotes 'one who is present as a witness." *Ash-Shahidul-Kamil* or perfect martyr is considered one who is killed in a religious war. The word *Shahid* is an Arabic word. It was given a wide interpretation in Muslim India. In *Qanoon-i-Islam* by Shreef different ways for the attainment of martyr-dom are mentioned which include the death while reciting prayers, death at the hands of robbers, death by lightning, death by drowning or falling in a dry well. But one who died in the defence of his faith was considered a perfect martyr. In Sikhism, the word *Shahid* was adopted in the sense of a perfect martyr. The Muslims who died in battle with infidels or Hindus were considered *Shahids.* But in Sikhism there is a wider connotation for the word *Shahid. A* Sikh who suffers death by refusing to renounce his faith, religion, tenet or principle or its practice is a *Shahid.* He seals his testimony for his faith with his blood.

Bhai Gurdas, while defining a true disciple, describes him as a martyr in endurance and faith, having ended all his illusions and fears. Once the Sikhs asked Guru Gobind Singh, "O True King, who may be called martyrs? Kindly tell us their nature of work." The Guru smiled and said, "You have put a question on a confidential matter, O Sikhs. The Guru keeps his people in his presence. He protects his disciples. The present is the dreadful Iron Age. The Guru is like a shepherd who cautions and scares away his followers. The Guru goads his Sikhs according to his will. If the Sikh has full faith, he is a hero of the field and crosses the world-ocean. The cowards are fettered in transmigration. The Guru shall wait alongwith his people. Whatever the martyrs desire, is fulfilled. God has placed many of them in responsible positions.... They wander in all the *Dvipas* and *Khandas,* but are never led astray. They see the sport of *maya,* but are not subject to transmigration. The Guru is there to protect them. He protects them like a shepherd.

## Martyrdom in Sikhism prior to eighteenth Century

The fifth Sikh Guru, Guru Arjan Dev was the first martyr in Sikh History. The Mughal Emperor Jahangir had himself ordered his death with tortures. He wrote in his *Tuzuk:* "So many of the simple-minded Hindus, many, many foolish Muslims too, had been fascinated by his ways and teachings. He was noised about as a religious and worldly leader. They called him Guru, and from all directions crowds of fool-world came to him and expressed great devotion to him. This busy traffic had been carried on for three or four generations. For years the thought had been presenting itself to my mind that either I should put an end to this false traffic, or he should be brought into the fold of Islam. . . . I fully knew his heresies, and I ordered that he should be brought into my presence, that his property be confiscated, and that he should be put to death with tortures." It is said that the Guru was handed over to Chandu Shah, who had also become inimical towards him because of a private matter. The adversary subjected the Guru to various kinds of tortures. Hot sand was poured over his body and he was made to sit on a hot iron-plate. The blistered body of the Guru was then put in the cold waters of the Ravi, which 'carried it away to its final rest.' The first martyrdom gave more strength to the Sikh movement. Guru Hargobind, the sixth Sikh Guru wore two swords of *miri* (temporal greatness) and *piri* (spiritual grandeur).

The second martyr in Sikh History was Guru Tegh Bahadur, the ninth Sikh Guru. The Mughal Emperor Aurangzeb tried to convert him to Islam, but the Guru remained steadfast on his principles. He gave his life in order to protect the freedom of the Hindu religion. In the words of Guru Gobind Singh: " He (Guru Tegh Bahadur) protected the forehead mark and sacred thread (of the Hindus), which marked a great event in the Iron Age. For the sake of saints, he laid down his head without even a sigh. For the sake of *Dharma* (righteousneess) he sacrificed himself; he laid down his head, but not his creed. The saints of the Lord abhor the performance of miracles and malpractices. Breaking the pot of his body on the head of the King of Delhi (Aurangzeb), he left for the abode of the

Lord. None could perform such a feat. The whole world bemoaned the departure of Tegh Bahadur, while the world lamented, the gods hailed his arrival in heaven." This martyrdom further strengthened the Sikh Movement. The Sikhs arrested with the Guru were also subjected to severe tortures. Bhai Mati DAs was sawth alive and Bhai Dayala was boiled in a huge cauldron.

## Eighteenth Century Martyrs

*Guru Gobind Singh—the first martyr of the Century*

The first martyr of the eighteenth century was Guru Gobind Singh, the tenth Guru of the Sikhs and the founder of the Khalsa. He had taken up the sword like his grandfather after the martyrdom of his father. His fight against the tyrants was for the spread of *Dharma* (Righteousness) and protection of the saints. He founded the Khalsa in order to root out the evil and evil-doers. For the accomplishment of his mission, he sacrificed his parents, himself and his sons. After the battle of Chamkaur, the Mughal forces pursued him closely for several days without any success. From Dina, he sent a letter entitled *Zafarnama* (Epistle of Victory) to Aurangzeb, in which he wrote, "Your army breaking the oath and in great haste, plunged in the battlefield with arrows and guns. For this reason, I had to intervene and had to come fully armed. When all other methods fail it is proper to hold the sword in the hand. . . . How could the brave ultimately withstand in the field, when only forty were surounded by innumerable warriors. . . . What, if you have killed my four sons, the hooded cobra still sits coiled up. . . ." Several Sikhs had laid down their lives in the battles of Bhangani, Nadaun, Anandpur etc. and had shown great feats in the battlefield. When the Guru left Anandpur, he was separated from a part of his family. His two younger sons Zorawar Singh and Fateh Singh alongwith their grandmother took shelter with an old servant, who betrayed them. He handed them over to the Muslim Governor of Sirhind. The Governor inhumanly tortured the young children and got them bricked alive. The grandmother could not survive because of the severe shock. Baba Ajit Singh and Bhai Udai Singh fought bravely on the banks of Sirsa, where Bhai Udai Singh fell in the field killing many enemies. Guru then encamped in the fortress of Chamkaur, where several brave warriors attained martyrdom in the battlefield alongwith Ajit Singh and Jujhar Singh, the two elder sons of the Guru. The Guru fought his last battle at Muktsar in Ferozepur district, in which the pursuing Mughal forces were defeated. The forty warriors of Majha, who had earlier deserted the ranks of the Guru during the siege of Anandpur, having been taunted by their womenfolk had reinforced the Guru's small army and attained martyrdom. They were blessed by the Guru and their 'disclaimer' was torn up. These forty are daily remembered in the Sikh prayer as *Chali Mukte*, the *Forty Saved Ones*.

On an invitation from Aurangzeb, the Guru started for Deccan, but the king died soon after and his son Bahadur Shah sought the help of the Guru. After defeating his adversaries, Bahadur Shah ascended the throne. The guilty Nawab of Sirhind, who had killed the two younger sons of the Guru, fearing the displeasure of the king on account of his friendship with the Guru, sent two Pathans who pursued the Guru, when he proceeded towards Deccan with the king. Finding an opportunity one day at Nander, one of the Pathans stabbed the Guru. Though the wounds of the Guru were healed within a few days after the attack, they burst open causing profuse bleeding when one day the Guru tried to bend a steel bow. The end of the worldly life of the Guru came on October 7, 1708. The line of the personal Guruship ended with this. The Guruship had been bestowed upon the *Adi Granth*.

Guru Gobind Singh was the third Guru to attain Martyrdom. The chain of martyrdoms following the death of the founder of the Khalsa within the eighteenth century is unique in the history of the world. The Khalsa moved fearlessly on the soil of Punjab, always keeping its head on its palm for the protection of truth, justice and righteousness. The tortures inflicted on the brave Khalsa were very severe, but the endurance and passive resistance of the mighty spirits was not lacking.

### The martyrdom of Banda Singh Bahadur

While in Deccan, Guru Gobind Singh himself had converted Banda Bairagi to Sikhism and had baptised him as Banda Singh. He was sent to Punjab with the object of punishing the evil-doers and tyrants. The Guru's objective was conveyed to the Sikhs in Punjab, who accepted Banda

78

Singh as their commander. Several successful battles were fought against the enemy. Khafi Khan says, "Not a man of the army of Islam escaped with more than his life and clothes he stood in. Horsemen and footmen fell under the swords of the infidels (forces of Banda Singh), who pursued them as far as Sirhind which was thereafter conquered and razed to the ground. Then after humiliating Gangetic Doab, the Sikh forces occupied Jullundur Doab. After that there was *Haidri Flag* crusade. The *mullas* of Lahore raised a green banner named *Haidri Flag* and proclaimed a crusade against the Sikhs. These *Ghazis* were ultimately defeated by the Sikh forces. Then the royal forces were called in. A fierce battle was fought at Lohgarh, after which the Sikh forces retreated towards the hills of Nahan.

Farrukh Siyarn became the king in the beginning of 1713 after internecine struggle in the royal family after the death of Bahadur Shah in 1712. During the reign of Bahadur Shah there were imperial orders for the extermination of the Sikhs. Farrukh Siyar appointed Abdus Samand Khan as the Governor of Lahore, who began to hunt the Sikhs everywhere. In the beginning of 1715 Banda Singh reappeared in the plains, his forces came under a siege in the fort of Gurdas Nangal. Because of the exhaustion of the provisions, Banda Singh and his men had to face heavy odds. Ultimately on December 7, 1715, Banda and his famished men were taken prisoners. At first they were taken to Lahore and then sent to Delhi. The execution of the Sikhs began on 5th March, 1716. It is said that one hundred Sikhs were executed every day. The author of *Siyarul-Mutaakhirin* says: "But what is singular, these people not only behaved firmly during the execution but they would dispute and wrangle with each other for priority in death, and they made interest with the executioner to obtain the preference." The carnage went on for a whole week. In the case of a newly married young man the mother appeared before the king requesting him to release her son as according to her, he was not a Sikh. The king granted her request, but when the orders for the release of the young man were presented before the Kotwal, the youngman cried out: "My mother is a liar, I am, undoubtedly, a Sikh." The turn of Banda Singh came on June 9, 1716. It is said that his son Ajai Singh, was hacked to death and cut into pieces before his very eyes and taking out the throbbing heart of the child, thrust it into the mouth of Banda 'who stood unmoved like a statue, completely resigned to the Will of God." As regards Banda

79

himself, he was deprived first of his right eye, then his left eye, after which his hands and feet were cut off. His flesh was torn with red-hot pincers and in the end his head was chopped off.

## Further Persecutions and Martyrdoms

After the death of Banda, a general order was issued by Farrukh Siyar that the Sikhs be completely extirpated. A reward was fixed for the head of a Sikh. The Sikhs wearing long hair, therefore, disappeared into hills and forests. When the situation eased a little, they came down on the plains. They used to assemble at Darbar Sahib, Amritsar on the occasion of Baisakhi and Diwali. Bhai Mani Singh became the head-priest of Darbar Sahib. In 1726, Abdus Samad Khan was transferred to Multan, and in his place Zakrya Khan, his son, known as 'Khan Bahadur' became the Governor of Lahore. Zakrya Khan adopted stronger measures for the extirpation of the Sikhs completely, so that the trouble on their account may end once for all. He fixed a price on the head of a Sikh. The Sikhs who came in the grip of the authorities, were given severe tortures in various ways. They were beheaded in public and their heads were piled up in *Shahid-Ganj* (treasure-troves of martyrdom) outside Delhi Gate. Having been outlawed, they again went away to the forests. According to Rattan Singh Bhangoo they had no hearths, no homes, no property, but they lived in the hope that one day they would be the rulers of the land. The other suppressed people still had sympathy for them and many of them joined the Khalsa brotherhood.

## Martyrdom of Tara Singh of Van

Tara Singh of Van was an ideal Sikh, a great public servant, audacious and bold. He was very popular with the Sikhs and fearlessly helped his brethren in distress. Sahib Rai of Noushera, living in the neighbourhood used abusive language for the Sikhs, when he was asked not to trespass his horses in the green fields of Tara Singh. The Sikhs, highly infuriated, caught and sold away one his mares. On the complaint from Sahib Rai, the Faujdar of Patti sent a detachment against Tara Singh, which was waylaid by the Sikh warriors in the way. Then the Faujdar requisitioned a larger force from the Governor of Lahore. Though Sardar

Tara Singh received a secret message from the Sikhs of Lahore but he refused to move to a safer place and died fighting bravely with the Mughal army alongwith his 22 men. The Sikhs vowed to wreak their vengeance for the onslaught and looted the revenue money meant for Government treasury. Under such circumstances of persecution and revenge, Zakrya Khan made a proposal to the Delhi Government that the Sikhs be given a grant and a title be conferred on their leader. After acceptance of this proposal, the Nawabship was conferred on Sardar Kapur Singh of Faisullapur. This gave a breathing time to the Sikhs. They organised themselves and the combined force of Budha Dal and Taruna Dal inflicted a heavy defeat on the Mughal army under the command of Lakhpat Rai.

## Martyrdom of Bhai Mani Singh

In 1738, Bhai Mani Singh was permitted to hold the Diwali festival in the Golden Temple on the condition that he would pay Rupees five thousand to the Government after the fair. In response to the invitation many Sikhs gathered. Since the forces entered the city (of Amritsar) during the fair, the Sikhs left in haste. The fair broke up. Bhai Mani Singh was arrested, because of the non-payment of the fixed amount. He was asked either to accept Islam or face death. The great Sikh savant refused to barter his religion. His body was hacked to pieces, limb by limb. A few companions also suffered martyrdom with him.

Because of the renewed persecutions, the Sikhs took shelter in the Shivalik hills. At this time, Nadir Shah devastated the land upto Delhi. After his departure, Zakrya Khan again launched an all-out campaign against the Sikhs. One Massa Ranghar took possession of the Golden Temple and turned the holy place into a dancing house. This desecration of the holy temple infuriated the Sikhs. Mehtab Singh and Sukha Singh disguised themselves as Muhammadans and entering the temple, cut off the head of the tyrant.

## Martyrdom of Bhai Taru Singh

Bhai Taru Singh aged twenty-five was a pious and devoted Sikh of village Poola of Majha. He worked in his fields and sent the produce to the common kitchen of his Sikh brethren. The Government considered it an act of treason. He was arrested and brought to Lahore. The tyrants tried to cut off his hair forcibly on the orders of Zakrya Khan. The hair had to be scraped off his scalp. This ordeal was faced by Bhai Taru Singh with great endurance. Zakrya Khan had died a few hours before him by a fatal disease.

## Martyrdom of Mehtab Singh of Mirankot, Subeg Singh and Shahbaz Singh

Mehtab Singh of Mirankot, who had killed Massa Ranghar, was captured and brought to Lahore and was publicly broken on the wheel on the orders of Zakrya Khan, who could not see the end of his other victims, who had been brought before him. These victims were Subeg Singh, an influential Zemindar of Jambar and his son Shahbaz Singh. The boy was a student in a Muhammadan school under a Qazi. The Qazi wished to convert the boy to Islam, but the boy refused. Then a charge was cooked up against him like Haqiqat Rai Dharmi (the virtuous) who suffered martyrdom eleven years earlier in 1734. Yahiya Khan, the son of Zakrya Khan, who became the Governor of Lahore after him, was also relentless and cruel like his father. He also got Subeg Singh arrested on a trumped up charge. He also refused to accept Islam. Both the father and son were bound to the wheel and turned on it. The slashing knives of the wheel finished both of them in a short while.

## The First Holocaust

Lakhpat Rai continued as Diwan under Yahiya Khan. When his brother Jaspat Rai, the Faujdar of Eminabad, was killed and the town was looted by the Sikhs, Lakhpat Rai became mad with rage. He got a general proclamation issued for the extirpation of the Sikhs. All the Sikhs of Lahore were arrested and executed. A huge Mughal army, under the command of Yahiya Khan and Lakhpat Rai pursued the Sikh warriors in the marshes of Kahnuwan and pushed them towards Ravi. After crossing the river, the Sikhs went towards the hills of Basohli, where they came under the attack of hillmen under the instruction from the Government. There was no other way left. They had either to take refuge in the steep mountain or to cut their way back through the advancing Mughal forces. Many Sikhs were killed and the others had to face great hardships. About

82

seven thousand were killed and three thousand were taken prisoners. The prisoners were subjected to great indignity and torture. In this campaign, the Sikhs suffered a heavy loss for the first time. It is therefore called a *ghalughara* or a holocaust. But it was a *Chhota ghalughara*, because the bigger one had yet to be experienced. This holocaust occurred in 1746.

In 1747, Yahiya Khan was ousted by his younger brother Shah Nawaz Khan, who put Lakhpat Rai into prison. The Mughal Government did not recognise Shah Nawaz as the Governor of Lahore. Therefore he invited Ahmed Shah Durrani, the ruler of Kabul, who reached Lahore in January 1748. Because of this new arrangement, the Sikhs got respite for some time. Dewan Kaura Mal was a Sikh at heart, therefore, there were no incidents of serious nature as long as he lived, except the siege of Ram Rauni, in which about two hundred Sikhs were killed.

Dewan Kaura Mal died in 1752 in an expedition against Durranis. Ahmed Shah Durrani had made the third excursion against the Mughals. Mir Mannu, feeling secure in his position as Governor of Lahore and seeing the rising power of the Sikhs, resorted to vigorous measures against them. On his orders about nine hundred Sikhs who had taken refuge in the fortress of Ram Rauni, were killed. The Sikhs were hunted and hammered to death with wooden clubs. Even the Sikh women were tortured and their children were cut to pieces before their very eyes. But none of them abandoned their religion. Hundreds of Sikh men and women were killed at *Shahid Ganj* outside Delhi Gate. A popular saying of the Sikhs of the period still abides, in which it is said, "Mannu is our sickle and we are a crop to be mowed by him; the more he cuts us, the more we grow." The tyrant himself was caught in the noose of death in November 1753. Then started the internecine struggles among the Muslim chiefs and further invasions of the Durrani. In this state of confusion. The Sikhs took advantage of the situation. The Durrani king had the upper hand because of the weakness of Delhi Government. He installed his son Taimur Shah as the Viceroy of Indian possessions. Because of their repeated excursions, a crusade was proclaimed against the Sikhs. There were losses on both sides.

The Sikh chiefs consolidated their power to an appreciable extent during the fifties and sixties of the eighteenth century, inspite of persecutions and skirmishes against them. It was during the sixth invasion of the Durrani king in February 1762, that the great holocaust or *wadda ghalughara* took place.

*Second Holocaust known as Wadda Ghalughara*

During the annual Diwali gathering at Amritsar in October, 1761 it was resolved that the strongholds of the supporters of the Durrani king be destroyed. In pursuance of this *gurmatta,* the nearest stronghold was that of the *Niranjanis* whose Guru Agil Das of Jandiala came to know of the Sikh resolve. Instead of making a compromise with the Sikhs, he invited the Durrani king, who was already on his way to India. The Sikhs withdrew hurriedly with their families and wanted to reach a safer place. The Shah pursued them and overtook them near Malerkotla, where nearly thirty thousand Sikhs hand encamped with their families and belongings. The orders were given for killing anyone in Indian dress. Several thousand Sikhs, mostly women and children were killed here. Those who survived kept moving further, while fighting, in order to save their families. They wanted to reach Barnala, but before they could reach there, their cordon was pierced by the invaders and a wholesale massacre followed. It is said that at least ten thousand Sikhs met their death in this carnage or *wadda ghalughara*. It is said that when the Shah returned to Lahore in the beginning of March, 1762, he brought with him fifty carts filled with the heads of the massacred Sikhs and a large number of captives. To punish the Sikhs further, he desecrated the Amritsar temple. The temple had also been desecrated earlier and the sacred tank had been filled up. The reports of such sacrilege had infuriated the Sikhs. Baba Deep Singh and Baba Gurbaksh Singh suffered martyrdom in 1760 in the battle of Ramsar in the city of Amritsar.

But the Sikhs recouped within a short period. They avenged the pollution of their most sacred places. Then followed a period of Sikh conquests and hearing about the Sikh victories, the Durrani king invaded India for the seventh time. The Sikhs moved away from the main route and went to Lakhi Jungle. But they did not completely absent themselves. There were several skirmishes with the Durrani forces during the stay of the Durrani king in India. It is said that he went to Chak Guru i.e. Amritsar to chastise the Sikhs there. But he did not find them there. There were about thirty Sikhs, who had been left in charge of *Akal Takht*. They were fearless persons. They sacrificed their lives for their Guru and every one

84

of them died a martyr.

After the return of the Shah in March 1765, the Sikhs assembled at Amritsar on the Baisakhi day and resolved to take possession of Lahore. This was done in the month of April. Thus the foundation of a Sikh kingdom was laid. The galaxy of martyrs had not only contributed for such a victory, but also glorified their great religion by their sacrifices. A great future cannot be denied to the people, whose history is full of the splendid feats of the martyrs.

The final touch be given to this short description of the Sikh Martyrs of the eighteenth century by a quotation of Bhagat Lakshman Singh, the author of *Sikh Martyrs:* "The Sikh martyrs, by a magic wand, as it were, completely metamorphosed the society and the country that gave them birth. They completely changed the course of events in the time in which they lived, falsifying the much-talked-of and much-commented upon theory that great men are mere products of their times. Men looked upon them with awe and wonder. The Sikh name acquired a new significance and new dignity."

# The Position of Woman in Sikhism

In Indian literature there is mention of several great women like Matreyi, Anusuya, Gargi, Arundati, Lilavati etc. In the Vedic period, the woman had both freedom and respect in society. She had equal opportunities with men in educational attainments and work. But there were times when she was considered much inferior to man. Some people gave her the status of the shoe of the foot of man. One of the periods of the downfall of the status of woman was the period of Muslim administration in India. Like the Muslim woman, the Indian (Hindu) woman was closeted in the four walls of her home. She was considered as the object of man's sexual satisfaction. The men of religion called her enchantress and thus condemned her. The Yogis considered her a "she-wolf". Tulsidas, the celebrated author of Ramacharit Manas dubbed her as worthy of warning and thus decried her. Peelu, an old Punjabi poet said, "It is a sin to look towards a woman even if she is made of paper". Generally we find the condemnation of women in this period. Some examples will not be out of place here. It is written in the Qissa of Mirza Sahiban written by Peelu:

Fie on the friendship of women, who are short of wisdom.
They enchant men with their smiles, but weep when questioned.

Similarly Muqbal in his Qissa "Heer Ranjha" has put the following lines in the mouth of Ranjha:

Ranjha says that there is no gain in meeting women,
No one should make friends with them
These women exhibit the True men as liars,
none should make a sacrifice for them.
The snakes do not hesitate to sting
Even if they are presented with milk at all times.

86

This tradition of the condemnation of women continued in Punjabi literature not only during Guru Nanak Age and the Later Mughal Period, but it is also seen in the poetry of Ranjit Singh Period and in the early British Period.

In this period of injustice with woman, we find her receiving full veneration in Gurmat Literature, the chief exponent of which is *Guru Granth Sahib*. It was Guru Nanak Dev, who first paid due regards to her and challenged those who condemned her with the remarks: "Why should we condemn her, who gives birth to kings". He says:

We are born of women, conceived by women and married to women. We befriend women and the Path continues through women. When one woman dies, we seek another, we are bound by women. Why should we talk ill of her, who gives birth to kings. The woman is born of woman, there is none without the female. There is only One Lord without the woman. (Var Asa M.1).

The very first savant of Gurmat, Bhai Gurdas, has defined woman as "Physically half and gate of salvation". In these words, there is not only latent the social significance of woman, but also the spiritual significance. During the period of the Sikh Gurus, the custom of *Sati* was prevalent in India. The woman burnt herself with her husband on the funeral pyre after his death. This was a type of suicide. Can it be imagined that she accepted her doom like a martyr? It was a great injustice with her that even not wanting such a death, she had to ascend the pyre for keeping up the folk-tradition. Guru Amar Das raised his voice against this horrible custom. He said:

They cannot be called *Satis*, who burn themselves with their dead husbands. They can only be called *Satis*, if they bear the shock of separation. They may also be known as *Satis*, who live with character and contentment and always show veneration to their husbands by remembering them. (Var Suhi M.3).

According to the Guru, the True wives of high character are the real *Satis*. Guru Arjan Dev has also expressed his views in this connection. He says:

One burns herself in the eyes of the world with the persistence of mind, but she cannot meet the Lord (in the next world) and instead undergoes many births and deaths. If she remains in character and continence and according to the will of her (dead) Lord, she can have no trouble in the world. She who has considered her Lord like God, blessed is such *Sati*, she receives approval in the Court of the Lord. (Gauri M.5).

Whereas, the woman of character has been called a *Sati* in the compositions of the Gurus, keeping in view the pitiable plight of a widow, the *bani* inspires the Hindu society for their reforms. If a young widow, under the impact of lust, surrenders herself to another person, she can never have the full satisfaction. She should take another husband and pass her life in satisfaction:

Just as a widow gives her body to another person, under the impact of lust and maya, she can never have satisfaction without a husband. (Gauri M.1).

In this way, Guru Nanak Dev has raised his voice in favour of re-marriage.

In the compositions of the Gurus, this fact has been clearly mentioned that God is the Creator of both man and woman, and He has Created all the relations. Therefore all have their own rights. For this reason, no prejudices should exist regarding the superiority or inferiority of any one. Guru Ram Das says:

The mother, father and sons are all Created by God;
The Lord Himself has fixed their relations.
(Gujri M.4).

There is no doubt about it that due to her physical weakness, the woman cannot do the same task as efficiently as man, but this does not mean that she is inferior to man. The world continues only through her creative work. Everyone has to perform his/her functions in a right manner.

The life of a woman is divided into three parts: as a daughter, as a wife and as a mother. For the daughter, the parents have certain responsibilities. The husband has certain responsibilities regarding his

88

wife and the children have certain responsibilities towards their mother. The stage of daughter is the stage of preparation. When she comes out of the age of playing with toys, she decks herself with qualities for the coming married life. At this stage she is always conscious about her future life and she is cautious about it. Guru Nanak Dev has expressed this state in the following way:

O damsel, do you not hear this news with your ears:
That you will have to come to your in-laws, you cannot remain always in your parents' home. (Sri Rag M.1).

Guru Arjan Dev gives his benediction to this damsel relating her life to both the homes of her parents and her in-laws:

Remember your Lord in your parents home and remain happy in the home of in-laws. Learn the qualitative way of living so that you may not experience any anguish. (Sri Rag M.5).

The testing-ground of the daughter is in the home of her in-laws. It is necessary that she should remain full of the fragrance of qualities. Guru Nanak Dev says:

There should be the toilet box of qualities, from which the fragrance may be drawn. O friend, if there are qualities, they should be shared. The qualities should be shared and the vices should be abandoned. Bedecking oneself with *such* silken raiments and other materials of qualities, one ought to get her due status. (Suhi M.1).

Absorbed in the love of the Lord, the beloved wife is decked with spontaneity and contentment and utters words full of love and reverence from her mouth:

1. Bedecked with spontaneity and contentment, she speaks sweetly (Sri Rag M.1).
2. · They speak sweetly, bow reverently and the Lord comes to their bed (Sri Rag M.3).

89

But the deserted woman always remains in agony, because she is always surrounded by vices:

The enchantress does not know any (useful) work; she is wicked and vicious. She does not get any peace in the homes of her parents and in-laws; she is burnt in falsehood and vices (Sri Rag M.1).

The *Suhagan* (beloved lady) has been portrayed by Guru Arjan Dev in the following manner:

She is virtuous and fortunate, blessed with sons, character and love of her Lord. She is beautiful, wise and sagacious, that lady is beloved of her Lord. She is high in character and status; she is ornamented with knowledge. Her clan and her brothers are eminent, and she is saturated with the love of her Lord. Her praise is inexpressible, who has been united and hugged by her Lord. Her Lord is Immortal, Unapproachable and non-phenomenal and she has the prop of love. (Majh M.5)

The greatness of this lady is indescribable. She is of great beauty and high character. She is full of qualities as a wife and very fortunate as a mother. Guru Arjan Dev has depicted an ideal woman in this way:

She is a lady of great accomplishments and qualities like Truth are her sons and other members of her family. She is obedient, wise and beautiful. Her Lord fulfils her wishes and she has done away with the vicious wives of the brothers of her Lord. She is the best of all her family members and puts the brothers of her Lord on the right path by her advice. Blessed is that home, where she manifests herself. There is peace and comfort in that house (Asa M.5).

This ideal woman is always absorbed in service. She enjoys the love of her Lord and is always busy in work. Guru Nanak Dev says in this connection:

Only then you can be called the ideal woman, if you do the appropriate work on the cloth and wear the shirt thus prepared. If you

90

care for your own home and do not fall in **vices, you** will be loved **by** your Lord. (Basant M.1).

This woman is a fine, significant and healthy constituent of society. No priceless object of the world attracts her except the love of her Lord. Multi-storeyed buildings, tasteful dishes, silken and soft beds, gold and silver have no attraction for her. If the Lord is with her, she feels peace and comfort on a stony bed, eating dry bread. The analogy of such a woman has been given to that devotee, who wins the Love of the Lord. Guru Arjan Dev has described the eminence of such a lady in the following words:

I sacrifice many comforts for a moment's union with the Lord during the night. I have no desire for a golden house with silken bed. All the pleasures inclusive of the possession of gems and pearls are futile without the Name of the Lord. And in the company of the Lord, the insipid dry food and sleeping on the earth appear comfortable. (Kanra M.5).

# Part II

# Guru Granth Sahib
## (The Sikh Scripture)

# I

# Guru Granth Sahib
# A Unique Scripture

The religious quest of man began with the origin of the human race. It took various forms: In earlier stages it manifested itself in magic, incantations and spells. It was followed by the belief in the power of spirits, ancestors, gods, totems and other divine beings. The worship of various gods and deities led to the concept of the One Highest Being under whose authority, various visible and invisible forces worked. This Supreme Being was All-Pervading, All-Powerful and All-Knowing. This Supreme Spirit was described in various ways and was regarded as the Supernatural Power controlling the activities of all the material and spiritual phenomenon in the universe.

The Enlightened Persons in various ages revealed their spiritual affinity with the Highest Being and recorded their experiences in the spiritual domain. They codified the injunctions for the visible man as well as the invisible man, presenting the divine discipline, for the welfare of humanity. Every nation which received these divine revelations was guided by them in succeeding centuries, setting its distinct tradition.

A Living Religion, thus has three distinct features. It has its own scripture, its own set of laws and a well-set tradition. Without these three factors, many religions which sprang up, have passed into oblivion. At present, there are eleven Living Religions in the world, four in the Indian sub-continent viz. Hinduism, Jainism, Buddhism and Sikhism, four in the Middle East i.e. Zoroastrianism, Judaism, Christianity and Islam, two in China viz. Taoism and Confucianism and one in Japan i.e. Shinto.

Sikhism is the youngest of world-religions. Its founder Guru Nanak Dev was born in A.D. 1469. He undertook four long journeys during his life and visited all the prominent centres of major religions. He held meaningful dialogues with the divines and savants of those religions and incorporated his thoughts in the hymns composed by him. The Sikh Scripture i.e. *Guru Granth Sahib*, which includes the compositions of the Sikh Gurus and the radical saints, is thus the acme and consummation of the religious and spiritual discipline. It contains the best of all religious ideals.

A brief account of the scriptures of other religions will not be out of place. The Sikh Gurus and the saints had great respect for all the religious systems and their scriptures. Kabir says, "Do not call the Vedas and the *Katebs* (Semitic scriptures) false; he, who does not reflect over them, is false." (p.1350, Prabhati Kabir). According to Guru Nanak Dev, all the four Vedas are truthful. Those who read and reflect upon them, have discriminatory thinking. (p.470, Var Asa M.1). Guru Amar Das says, "The world is burning, O Lord, Be Compassionate and Save it. Redeem it, through whichever gate it comes unto You." (p.853, Var Bilawal M.4, Shalok M.3). The Gates mentioned by Guru Amar Das are the Religions of the World.

The scriptures of Hinduism consist of *Shruti* and *Smriti*. The four Vedas viz. Rig, Sama, Yajur and Atharva are the *Shruti* or the revealed texts. The *Smritis* include *Itihasas* and *Puranas*. The two great epics i.e. *Ramayana* and *Mahabharata* are *Itihasas*. There are eighteen *Maha-Puranas* and eighteen *Upa-Puranas*. The Vedas consist of Mantras, Brahmanas, Aranayakas and Upanishads. The Brahmanas contain the rituals; the Aranayakas are the forest-treatises. Upanishads are the most important part of the Vedas. They are the exponents of Vedanta or the religious philosophy of the Vedas. Bhagavad Gita forms part of *Mahabharata*. The Vedas are said to have been composed between 2000 B.C. and 1000 B.C. The Vedic Mantras are invocations to various gods.

The Buddhist scriptures consist of *Ti-Pitaka* (Three Baskets) and the *Dhammapada*. The three Baskets are the *Vinaya Pitaka*, which deals with the duties for the monks and nuns, the *Sutta Pitaka*, which contains the doctrines in the forms of sermons, parables and proverbs, and the *Abhidhamma Pitaka*, which contains the abstruse Buddhist philosophy and explanations of Buddhist doctrines and psychology. The Dhammapada consists of a collection of the sayings of Lord Buddha.

The three important *Agamas* or scriptures of Jainism are *Akaranga Sutra, Sutrakritanga* and *Uttaradhyayana Sutra*. They contain the precepts of Jainism. The *Akaranga Sutra* deals with the Jaina conduct.

96

The Sutrakritanga refuting the heretical doctrines, discusses the holy life to be led by a Jaina monk and the punishments to be accorded for the unholy life. The *Uttaradhyayana Sutra* instructs the Jaina monk regarding his duties. The knowledge about the animate and inanimate things is given to him.

The sacred writings of Zoroastrianism are collectively called *Zend-Avesta*. The fragments which are available include the *Gathas* or psalms, said to have been composed by Zoroaster himself, the *Visperad*, often employed in worship services, the *Vendidad*, a priestly code, containing also the theology, cosmology and history of the religion and the *Yashts*, a series of hymns.

The scriptures of Judaism include the *Torah* or the Book of Moses, depicting the "Law", the *Nevi'im*, consisting of the books of the "Prophets," and the *Ketubim* i.e. "Writings", containing mainly the Books of Wisdom. These books are collectively called the Old Testament.

The scripture of Christianity is called the *New Testament*, in which are grouped together *Four Gospels*, relating the Life and Sayings of Jesus Christ, *a Book of Acts*, manifesting the development of the belief in Lord Christ in a religious movement, the *Epistles*, written by Saint Paul and other missionaries and the *Ravelation*, a book of divine visions. The Jewish scriptures were also accepted as the sacred writings of Christianity, because of the birth of Jesus Christ as a Jew and the predictions about him in the Jewish scriptures.

The scripture of Islam is the *Koran*, which consists of 114 chapters called *suras*. The first *sura* contains a short prayer. Each *sura* is complete in itself like the psalm in the Bible (New Testament). In the remaining 113 *suras*, the longer ones come first and the shorter ones come later. These *suras* are grouped in thirty *siparahas*. The scripture consists of revelations vouchsafed to Prophet Muhammad.

The sacred writings of Taoism include the *Tao Teh King* and the writings of Chuang-Tze. The *Tao Teh King* is the basic scripture. It is mostly ethical in content and consists of wise sayings and generalizations. The writings of Chuang-Tze contain three parts viz. the *Nei* (Inner), the *Wai* (Outer) and the *Ta* (Miscellaneous). The first part contains seven books, the second fifteen books and the third eleven. The significant doctrines of the religion and its esoteric teachings are contained in the first

97

part. The remaining two parts are supplementary.

The scriptures of Confucianism consist of the *Shu King* (Book of History), the *Shi King* (Book of Poetry), the *I King* (Book of Changes), the *Li Ki* (Book of Rites), the *Ch' un Ch' iu* (Spring and Autumn Annals), the *Hsiao King* (Book of Filial Piety), the *Ta Hsio* (Great Learning), the *Chung Yung* (Doctrine of the Mean), the *Lun Yu* (Analects) and the *Meng-tze* (Book of Mencius). The first six scriptures are called the Classics, which are said to have been compiled by Confucius himself. The remaining four were added by later generations.

Shinto, the national religion of Japan is called *Kami-no Michi* (The Way of the gods). Its sacred writings are *Kojiki* (Records of Ancient Matters) and *Nihongi* (Chronicles of Japan). The first work tell the story of the gods before the creation of men and also of the early emperors. The second work consists of the stories of the emperors of Japan. *Engishiki* (Institutes of the Period of Engi), another sacred work contains the story of the rise of Shinto religion as well as twenty-five prayers for ceremonial occasions. Another sacred work of Shinto Faith in *Manyoshu* (Collection of Ten Thousand Leaves) which is an anthology of poems.

Besides *Guru Granth Sahib*, the second scripture of Sikhism is the *Dasam Granth* or the Book of the Tenth Master. The scholars are divided over the authorship of several compositions included in it. The poems like JAP SAHIB, AKAL USTAT, SHABAD HAZARE, SWAYYAS, GYAN PRABODH, SHASTAR NAM MALA. The autobiographical portion and *Chandi Charitras* alongwith *Var Durga ki* in BACHITTAR NATAK and ZAFAR NAMA are considered the compositions of Guru Gobind Singh, while other poems like CHAUBIS AVATAR, TRIYA CHARITTAR, HIKAYATS etc. as the compositions of the court poets of the Tenth Master. According to Kesar Singh Chhibbar, as recorded in his *Bansawali Nama*, the Guru refused to include his poems in *Guru Granth Sahib*, considering them as a poetic pastime.

There are several points on which *Guru Granth Sahib* differs from the other scriptures of the world:

1. *Guru Granth Sahib* is purely monotheistic. It accepts only One God and rejects all other deities, spirits, angels etc. Only God is Immortal. All the other deities are mortal and prone to death. "Why should we (remember and) serve others, who undergo

98

birth and death." (p.509, Var Gijri M.3). "He neither has father nor mother, nor sons, nor brothers" (p.1021, Maru M.1). "He does not seek the advice of another and Does All by Himself whatever He wants to Do." (p.863, Gond M.5). Thus *Guru Granth Sahib* does not believe like the New Testament in the Son of God and in a Prophet like the Holy Quran.

·2.  *Guru Granth Sahib* being free from inhibitions of any kind regarding the way of life and its adaptability in all the regions of the world vouches its universality. It is not a religion of the chosen people (like Judaism), but, instead, it is the religion of the entire humanity. It rises above all the regional barriers. "The True Guru wishes the well-being of all the creation" (p.302, Var Gauri M.4).

3.  *Guru Granth Sahib* rejects all ritualism, formalism and symbolism. The adherents of most of the religions perform various rites and ceremonies in order to appease their deities or achieve their objectives. Thus the priestcraft is rejected. All the intermediaries, exploiting the masses in the name of religion, have been brought under severe criticism. *Guru Granth Sahib* has no belief in any sacrament.

4.  *Guru Granth Sahib* focusses all its attention on the unfoldment of the discipline for the attainment of the unity of the *jiva* with Brahman. The emphasis has been laid on the adoption of godly qualities by the seeker.

5.  *Guru Granth Sahib* repudiates the prevalent theories of creation and scans the universe as the work of the Creator, whose existence pulsates everywhere in His Creation. All the beliefs regarding the origin of creation are wrong. The extent and expanse of the Creation of the Infinite Lord cannot be delimited. The created phenomena, from the minutest to the greatest, is under the Surveillance of the Lord.

6.  *Guru Granth Sahib* lays great emphasis on honest and sincere labour. Its religion is the religion of workers and house-holders. Therefore, it decries the renunciation and all types of ascetic practices.

7.  *Guru Granth Sahib* advocates the equality of all human beings, irrespective of birth and sex. The woman is, in no way, inferior

to man. *Guru Granth Sahib* rejects all distinctions of caste and colour. The *Varnashrama Dharma* of Hinduism, propagating the distinctions of caste and advocating various stages of life, has been bitterly criticised. The untouchability, thus, becomes a slur on society.

8. The State has to play its part in the provision of food, shelter and clothing to the members of the society. There can be no devotion, if the individual is not carefree about his requirements.

9. *Guru Granth Sahib* presents a balanced combination of action *(Karma)*, devotion *(Bhakti)* and knowledge *(Gyan)*. It is essentially a religion of Devotion. Whereas the body has to work for the well-being of the family and society, the mind has to remain in tune with the Lord. Service is, thus, the motto of an adherent of *Guru Granth Sahib*. His best service towards the Guru and the Lord is the remembrance of the Name. One must also share his earnings (preferably *Tithe*) with the deserving and needy. The core of the teaching of *Guru Granth Sahib* is *Nam Japna* (remembrance of the Name of the Lord), *Kirt Karni* (The honest labour) and *Wand Chhakna* (Sharing of the earnings).

10. The religion of *Guru Granth Sahib* is most practical. The devotee overbrims with love and devotion. He visualises the Lord all around him in multifarious forms and guises. The whole world appears as a family to him. The Earth is an abode of *Dharma* for him. He passes his whole life under the dense shade of his Guru, who is Dharma-incarnate.

THE UNIQUE ASPECT OF GURU GRANTH, as compared with other scriptures of the world, is its unique position, as an embodiment of the Spirit of the Ten Sikh Gurus and the Saints, Whose WORD is included in it. It is the SHABAD GURU. "THE BOOK IS THE ABODE OF GOD" (p.1226, Sarang M.5). It is the Guru (Preceptor) for all times. Guru Gobind Singh, the tenth and the last Sikh Guru circumambulated and bowed his head before it, thereby ending the line of personal Guruship. Since A.D. 1708, it has attained the position of the "Eternal Guru". It receives veneration and shall ever receive veneration like the "LIVING GURU". No living Guru can take its place. Its WORD directs the devotee in all his functions, the secular as well as the spiritual.

## II

# Compilation of Guru Granth Sahib

The compilation of *Guru Granth Sahib* began, when Guru Nanak Dev, during his travels, undertook to collect the *bani* (hymns) of the like-minded saints in his Note-book called *"Pothi"*. A mention of this *Pothi* has been made in *Puratan Janamsakhi*. This *Pothi* was passed on to the second Pontiff, Guru Angad Dev, when the Guruship was bestowed on him. We cannot say with certainty the names of the saints whose verses were included in it, because it could not be preserved. During his travels, Guru Nanak Dev might have collected the hymns of Kabir and Ravidas in Uttar Pradesh, of Jaidev in Bengal, of Namdev in Maharashtra and of Sheikh Farid in Punjab. It seems probable on the basis of the *Pothis* of Baba Mohan, one of whose source for compilation must have been the *Pothi* of Guru Nanak Dev, which must have been received by Guru Amar Das, the third Guru from the second Pontiff.

We find mention of the four *Pothis* of Baba Mohan, two of which have been preserved and the other two have been lost. Baba Mohan the son of Guru Amar Das was in the possession of these *Pothis*, when the fifth Guru, Guru Arjan Dev compiled *Granth Sahib*. The Guru went himself to take these Pothis, which were ultimately handed over to him, though hesitantly. These manuscripts were prepared earlier under the personal supervision of Guru Amar Das, by his grandson Sahansar Ram. One of the available manuscripts is at Patiala and the other at Ahiyapur, District Hoshiarpur. The first manuscript contains 300 leaves and the second 224. Every leaf contains 13 lines and every line about thirteen words. The first manuscript begins with Suhi Raga and the second with Ramkali Raga. Both the manuscripts together contain the hymns in fifteen Ragas. At the end of each Raga, the *bani* of the saints is given. It seems evident that the *bani* of other Ragas had been included in the other two manuscripts, which have been lost. Gyani Gyan Singh, the author of *Twarikh Guru*

*Khalsa*, according to his statement, had seen one of these manuscripts beginning with Sri Raga.

The compilation of the *bani* of Guru Nanak Dev and the like-minded saints was Herculian task for Guru Arjan Dev. The *bani* of Guru Angad Dev, Guru Amar Das and Guru Ram Das had been preserved in the House of the Guru, but the *bani* of Guru Nanak Dev lay scattered far and wide, because of the extensive travels of the Guru. The Guru had been reciting and singing his bani before his audience at various places, which he visited during his travels, and the Sikhs accompanying him had been putting it in black and white. Names of several such persons have been mentioned in *Puratan Janamsakhi* e.g. Bhai Mansukh, Bhai Bhagirath, Hassu Lohar, Saido Gheo, and Sheehan Chhimba. Several devotees at distant places had preserved his *bani*, which they had been reciting and singing in their congregations. Undoubtedly, the Guru had written some of his hymns and those of the saints in his *Pothi*, but a large portion of his verses and those of the saints had still to be collected. A *Hukamnama* (An Order) of the fifth Guru was circulated to all the Sikh centres, both inside and outside the country, for the collection of the *bani* of Guru Nanak Dev.

The Sikh Sangats of far and near, complying with the orders of the fifth Guru, sent the compositions of Guru Nanak preserved by them. The Guru sent Bhai Paira (most probably Paira Mokha, who was the scribe of *Bhai Bale Wali Janamsakhi)* to Ceylon for bringing the compositions of Guru Nanak Dev bound in a collection entitled "Pran Sangali". It is recorded in Sikh Chronicles that Bhai Paira succeeded in bringing the manuscript from Mayadunne, the grandson of Shivnabh, who had become a great devotee of Guru Nanak Dev.

Guru Nanak Dev and his successors had composed their verses under the Name "Nanak". In order to differentiate the verses of each Guru, the serial number of Guruship was mentioned with them adding the word *Mahla* which connotes "the wife of the Lord". Since the religion of Guru Nanak Dev was spreading far and wide, the hymns of the Gurus were becoming popular day by day. There were several others in those days, who were passing out their verses with the name "Nanak", therefore it was a huge task to separate the real verses from the false ones. Since the hymns under the name "Nanak" were increasing in time, the Sikhs requested Guru Arjan Dev to select the genuine verses of Guru Nanak Dev for them. It was very difficult for them to discriminate between the genuine and the false verses. It was at their request that the idea of *Granth Sahib* originated. While Guru Arjan Dev was at work selecting the real verses of Guru Nanak Dev, he thought of the compilation of *Granth Sahib* for the Sikhs. In this way, he preserved the poetry of his predecessors and other saint-poets for posterity.

It is said that the elder brother of Guru Arjan Dev, Prithi Chand by name, had also been trying to compose and get composed hymns and pass them out as those of Guru Nanak and other Gurus. In this way he wanted to be recognised as the Guru. This also led Guru Arjan Dev to prepare an anthology of poetry of the preceding Sikh Gurus along with his own compositions. According to Kesar Singh Chhibbar, as recorded in his *Bansavali Nama*, the son of Prithi Chand, Meharvan, having been a poet, began to compose verses under the name "Nanak". Prithi Chand and his followers, known as *Meenas* got a *Granth* prepared in which they included the hymns of the first four Gurus. In order to establish the Gurudom of Prithi Chand, the bards began to sing the hymns composed by Meharvan. One day Guru Arjan Dev heard a hymn of Meharvan being sung by the bards. He told Bhai Gurdas that the genuine hymns be separated from the false ones because the *Meenas* were mixing them up. This was the beginning of the compilation of the *Granth Sahib*. This fact has been recorded by Kesar Singh Chhibbar in his *Bansavali Nama* in the following manner:

"Meharvan, the son of Prithia (Prithi Chand) used to compose Poetry. He studied Persian, Hindvi, Sahaskriti and Gurmukhi. He composed a lot of poetry putting the name of Guru Nanak at the end of his poems. The Dooms (Minstrels) began to sing the hymns of *Meenas* (Prithi Chand and his followers). They created another Guruship. These Meenas got prepared a *Granth* (holy book) and interspersed the hymns of the first four Gurus. The Purohits and Brahmins took sides, some to this side and some to that. Those who went to the other side were inimical to those belonging to this side. Those who came to this side left their (those of the other side) Court. . . . Here the Sikh *Rababis* were employed for *Kirtan* (Congregational singing). Some Sikh recited here a hymn composed by Meharvan, which was heard by Guru Arjan Dey. He said to Bhai Gurdas, "The hymns of the Gurus must be separated. The *Meenas*

103

are going to mix up hymns, which should be set in order". The Guru had been composing the hymns in the past, which were gathered together by Bhai Gurdas.

Bhai Gurdas was the scribe, who wrote *Granth Sahib* in Gurumukhi script, which was one of the prevalent scripts in Punjab in those days. Some people believe that the *Gurmukhi* script was prepared by Guru Angad Dev, the second Sikh Guru. There is no doubt that its name Gurmukhi was coined at that time, but the poem "Patti" of Guru Nanak Dev, which consists all the letters of Gurmukhi script is a clear proof of its remote origin. Bhai Gurdas while scribing the *Guru-bani* in the *Granth Sahib* wrote all the words of a verse together and did not divide them off in pursuance of the practice in the ancient scripts, therefore the novice feels it a bit difficult to read a verse, which looks like a big word. Sometimes without a proper guide, a verse becomes a puzzle for the beginner. Although nowadays several printed editions of the *Adi Granth* are available in which the words have been divided off, but still the versions of the verses may be doubtful. The distinctive use of i and u in *Guru Granth Sahib* has led some Sikh scholars to prepare its Grammar.

Guru Arjan Dev collected all the material for the *Granth Sahib*, which came through several sources. The bards had left their panegyrics with the Gurus, whom they had met in their lives. The hymns of Guru Nanak Dev had been collected from far and near. The hymns of the succeeding Gurus had been there in the House of the Guru. The hymns of the like-minded saints had been collected from their followers, though some of the hymns had been included in the Pothis of Guru Nanak and Baba Mohan. The saints had been travelling extensively within the length and breadth of India. The Maharashtrian saint Namdev is said to have visited Punjab during his lifetime. There is a shrine in his name at village Ghuman of Gurdaspur district. Several other saints like Kabir, Ravidas, etc. had been intimately known to the people of Punjab through their devotees and popular hymns. The Bhakti Movement had gained great momentum in this area because of the work being done by the Sikh Gurus. The popularity of the saints like Namdev, Kabir, Ravidas, Sain and Trilochan can be well-imagined through the verses of the third, fourth and fifth Sikh Gurus, e.g.

1.  Namdev, the calico printer and Kabir, the weaver attained final emancipation through the True Guru. (p.67, Sri Rag M.3).

2.  Namdev, Jaidev, Trilochan, Kabir and Ravidas, the low-caste tanner,
    And Dhanna, the Jat and Sain (the barber), all met God, repairing to the feet of the Saints. (p.835, Bilawal M.4)

3.  In the Iron age (Kaliyuga), the Name of the Lord is most efficacious; it emancipates all the devotees;
    Were not all the woes of Namdev, Jaidev, Kabir, Trilochan and Ravidas, the tanner, completely dispelled? (p.995, Maru M.4).

4.  The mind of Namdev became attuned with the Lord,
    That calico-printer of little worth became very precious.
    Forsaking his spinning and weaving, Kabir cherished the love of the Feet of the Lord,
    That weaver of low lineage, became the treasure of qualities.
    Ravidas, who always carted the dead animals, abandoned maya;
    He became renowned in the company of the saints and had the sight of the Lord.
    Sain, the barber, and common servant, became known in every house,
    He enshrined the Lord in his heart and was counted among the Bhaktas (Devotees).
    Hearing all this, Dhanna, the Jat, was absorbed in devotion,
    The Lord appeared before him, Dhanna was so fortunate.
    (p.487-88, Asa M.5).

These examples from the verses of the Sikh Gurus exhibit their great veneration for the Bhaktas, whose verses were included in the *Granth Sahib*. Even Kabir has praised the devotion of Jaidev and Namdev (p.856) and Ravidas has appreciated Namdev, Kabir, Trilochan, Sadna and Sain. This shows that throughout the northern India, all the above-mentioned saints were reverently mentioned in every house. Therefore, Guru Arjan Dev, while compiling the *Granth Sahib* procured the hymns of the saints from the followers of the saints within Punjab or the surrounding areas. Even when the living saints came to know about the preparation of *Granth*

*Sahib*, they came to meet the Guru and requested him to include their hymns also in the holy Granth. In the biography of the Guru, mention has been made of four such saints coming from Lahore namely Peelu, Chhajju, Kahna and Shah Hussain.

# III

# Editing of Guru Granth Sahib

After compiling the material from different sources for *Granth Sahib*, having engaged four scribes namely Sant Das, Haria, Sukha and Mansa Ram according to Kesar Singh Chhibbar (as mentioned in his *Bansavali Nama*), Guru Arjan Dev started the work of editing the great scripture within the bounds of Ramsar in Amritsar. The compilation work had been finished in A.D. 1601 and for the next three years, the work of editing was done and completed in A.D. 1604. The scribe was Bhai Gurdas, the great Sikh savant and poet. As has been hinted earlier, the work of compilation and editing had been prompted by the fake *bani* prepared by the Meenas (Prithi Chand and his family). According to Kesar Singh Chhibbar, "Meharvan, the son of Prithi Chand (the elder brother of Guru Arjan Dev) began to compose verses under the name of Nanak. Prithi Chand and his followers got a Granth prepared in which they included the hymns of the first four Gurus. In order to establish the Gurudom of Prithi Chand, the bards began to sing the hymns composed by Meharvan. One day Guru Arjan Dev heard a hymn of Meharvan being sung by the bards. He told Bhai Gurdas that the genuine hymns be separated from the false ones because the Meenas were mixing them up". Thus began the compilation and editing of the *Granth Sahib*. The Guru had been composing the hymns in the past, which were gathered together by Bhai Gurdas. The script used by Bhai Gurdas was Gurmukhi. Some people believed that the Gurmukhi script was prepared by Guru Angad Dev, the second Sikh Guru, when the original biography of Guru Nanak Dev was scribed by Paira Mokha. But the poem entitled Patti, composed by Guru Nanak Dev contains all the letters of Gurmukhi, which is a clear proof of its remote origin.

### Touchstone for the selection of hymns for the *Adi Granth:*

The very first consideration for the inclusion of the hymns of various saints for the new anthology was the ideology of Guru Nanak Dev. Some of the hymns of like-minded saints had already been collected by Guru Nanak Dev in his *Pothi* and Guru Amar Das in *Baba Mohan dian Pothian*. Guru Arjan Dev had even dropped some of the hymns of the saints already compiled. Seven hymns of Kabir and two of Namdev, included in Baba Mohan dian Pothian have not been included in *Guru Granth Sahib*. (See *Sri Kartarpur di Bir de Darshan*--by Bhai Jodh Singh). The thoughts of the contemporary saints like Kahna, Peelu, Chhajju and Shah Hussain were not in consonance with the ideology of Guru Nanak Dev, therefore the hymns of these saints were not accepted. A large number of Shalokas composed by the Gurus were interspersed in longer poems especially Vars of the Gurus. Some Shlokas were appended with the Shlokas of Kabir and Farid for clarification and elaboration. The Yogic path of Pranayama and Asanas was not acceptable to Guru Nanak Dev, therefore the compositions of Gorakhnath and his disciples were left out and not considered at all. The saints who were traditionalists and believed in Karma Kanda and Upasana Kanda were also not considered. The compositions included in *Pran-Sangali* and said to be the work of Guru Nanak Dev was closely scrutinised and everything connected with Hathyoga was left out from the purview of selection.

Another criterion besides the ideology was that of Ragas and Raginis (musical modes). Only *Japuji* in the beginning and Shlokas and Swayyas at the end of the anthology are free from any musical notation. The main body of the scripture has been divided into musical modes. The order of the poetry included in *Guru Granth Sahib* is as follows:-

*I Part:*  (a)  Japuji of Guru Nanak Dev, which is the morning prayer of the Sikhs.

        (b)  Rahiras—the evening prayer—containing the following order of hymns:

1. So Daru Raga Asa Mahla I
2. Asa Mahla I
3. Asa Mahla I

4. Gujri Mahla IV
5. Gujri Mahla V
6. So Purukh Asa Mahla IV
7. Asa Mahla IV
8. Asa Mahla I
9. Asa Mahla V

(c) Sohila—the bed-time prayer contains the hymns in the following order:

1. Gauri Deepki Mahla I
2. Asa Mahla I
3. Dhanasari Mahla I
4. Gauri Purbi Mahla IV
5. Gauri Purbi Mahla V

The hymns in (b) and (c) are drawn from Ragas in part II.

*II Part:* It contains hymns of the Gurus and saints in the following thirty-one Ragas and Raginis:-

1. Sri Raga
2. Majh
3. Gauri
4. Asa
5. Gujri
6. Devgandhari
7. Bihagra
8. Vadhans
9. Sorath
10. Dhanasari
11. Jaitsri
12. Todi
13. Bairari
14. Tilang
15. Suhi
16. Bilawal
17. Gaund

18. Ramkali
19. Nat Narain
20. Mali Gaura
21. Maru
22. Tukhari
23. Kedara
24. Bhairo
25. Basant
26. Sarang
27. Malar
28. Kanra
29. Kalyan
30. Prabhati and
31. Jaijavanti.

In these Ragas and Raginis, the following order of hymns is observed:

1. *Chaupade, Dupade, Tipade, Panchpade* or *Chhipade* with the number of musical notation of the Raga/Ragini in serial order and the number of *Mahla* in serial order.

2. *Ashtapadis* with the number of musical notation of the Raga/Ragini in serial order and the number of *Mahla* in serial order.

3. *Solhe*, if any, with the number of *Mahla* in serial order.

4. Poems with special sub-headings with the number of *Mahla* and musical notation in serial order, which do not come under 1 and 2.

5. Chhants with the number of musical notation and the number of *Mahla* in serial order.

6. Vars of the Gurus in serial order followed by Var written by bards, if any

7. The hymns of the saints, mostly beginning with Kabir, followed by Namdev, Ravidas and other saint-poets.

*III Part:* Shlokas and Swayyas are given in the following order:

1. Sahaskriti Shlokas
2. Gatha Shlokas

110

3. Phunhay
4. Chaubolay
5. Shlokas of Kabir
6. Shlokas of Sheikh Farid
7. Swayyas of Guru Arjan Dev
8. Swayyas written by bards as panegyrics on the first, second, third, fourth and fifth Gurus in serial order.
9. Shlokas in excess of Vars by the first, third, fourth and fifth Gurus in serial order.
10. Shlokas of the Ninth Guru.
11. *Mundavani* (The Seal) consisting of two Shlokas.
12. Ragamala.

Guru Arjan Dev used to compose hymns for inclusion in *Granth Sahib* at the time of editing. It is said, when *Basant ki Var* was being composed, the Guru was requested by the servant to take meal. The Guru rose, when only three Pauris had been written. The incomplete Var without even the Shlokas interspersed before the Pauris was included in *Granth Sahib*.

**Three Recensions of *Guru Granth Sahib*:**

The original volume of *Granth Sahib* prepared by Guru Arjan Dev, with the scribe Bhai Gurdas, was installed by the Guru at the Darbar Sahib (Golden Temple) at Amritsar, when it was complete. Baba Budha was the first high-priest *(Granthi)*. This recension passed on from Guru Arjan Dev to Guru Hargobind and to his grandson Dhir Mal, the son of Baba Gurditta. Har Rai, the brother of Dhir Mal became the Guru who thought it advisable to take possession of *Granth Sahib*. Thenceforward, this recension remained in the family of Dhir Mal at Kartarpur and is still there. It is, therefore, known as *"Kartarpur wali Bir"*.

The second recension is known as *"Bhai Banno ki Bir"*, which was prepared, when Bhai Banno was taking the first recension for binding at Lahore. This second recension contains two additional hymns—one of Sur Das and the other of Mira Bai and several other poems after *Mundavani* (the Seal). Guru Arjan Dev did not approve of the additions of Bhai Banno and are thus considered apocryphal. This second recension is called *Khari*

111

*Bir*, which is still with the descendants of Bhai Banno.

When Dhir Mal was approached by Guru Gobind Singh to give *Granth Sahib*, he did not care for the request, but instead said tauntingly: "If you are the Guru, you prepare your own". The Guru had been busy in the battlefield for a long time. He had no human successor in view. He wanted to bestow Guruship on *Granth Sahib*. Therefore, when he left Anandpur, he stayed at Damdama Sahib for some time. Bhai Mani Singh joined him there and worked as a scribe for the third recension. The Guru dictated and Bhai Mani Singh wrote. As the story goes, it was a miraculous feat, but it appears that a manuscript copy of the first recension was provided to him by the Sikhs. In this third recension, the additions made in the first recension are the hymns of the ninth Guru. In the Shlokas of the ninth Guru at the end of the holy Granth, there is one Shloka said to have been composed by Guru Gobind Singh himself.

The poetry of Guru Gobind Singh was later on collected by Bhai Mani Singh in one volume and named *Dasam Granth*. It is said that Guru Gobind Singh was asked by the Sikhs to include his compositions in *Granth Sahib*, but he refused saying that The *Guru Granth Sahib* was the genuine Granth and his poetry was merely a poetic sport, therefore it could not be included in that genuine Granth. This third recension is known as *Damdame wali Bir*. This is the complete recension of Granth Sahib. Guru Gobind Singh bestowed Guruship on it and thereby ended the line of personal Guruship.

# IV

## The Composers of the Divine Poetry
## of the Adi Granth

It has been said of the Bible: "Human creatures took over the actual work of writing, but they all wrote under God's guidance and dictation, being moved by His Spirit. Some were judges and kings. Some were learned, others were lowly labourers, herdsmen, fishermen etc. They were not professional writers, but men of action, servants and witnesses of Jehovah from all walks of life. They wrote over long stretch of years. . . ."[1] The same can be said of *Guru Granth Sahib*. Guru Nanak Dev has plainly said:

Whatever Word I receive from the Lord,
I pass it on in the same strain, O Lalo!

Thus the Word of God has been put forth in *Guru Granth Sahib*. The contributors were all types of men: Jaidev was a Brahmin, Pipa was a king, Namdev was a calico-printer, Trilochan was a Vaish, Sadhna was a butcher, Dhanna was a farmer, Sain was a barber, Kabir was a weaver, Ravidas was a cobbler and the Gurus were all Kshatriyas. They all composed the divine songs over a stretch of about six centuries. Jaidev, the Bengali saint of the twelfth century, is the oldest composer included in this holy book. Namdev, the famous Maharashtrian poet, belonged to the fourteenth century. Kabir, the Hindi poet of the Gangetic valley, flourished in the fifteenth century. Guru nanak Dev and his successors lived in the sixteenth nd seventeenth centuries.

1.  JAIDEV                    Two hymns in the *Guru Granth Sahib*

Jaidev was born at Kenduli in the district of Birbhum, Bengal. The dates of his birth and death are not known. It is said that he was one of the five distinguished poets of the court of Lakshman Sen, the King of Bengal, who dates from A.D. 1170. The name of his father was Bhojdeva and that of his mother Bamadevi. He is the author of famous Sanskrit poem *Gita Govinda*. He was married to Padmavati, the daughter of an Agnihotri Brahmin of Jagannath. His dedication and devotion to the Lord was so great that the Lord himself came to complete one of the hymns, which the saint could not

2.  SHEIKH FARID    Four hymns and 130 Shlokas

Sheikh Farid or Farid Shakearganj, a Sufi was born at Khotwal in west Punjab in A.D.1173. The name of his father was Sheikh Jamal-ud-Din Suleiman and that of his mother was Miriam. He was married to the daughter of Ghias-ud-Din Balban, a king of the Slave dynasty. He had five sons and three daughters. He was the disciple of Khwaja Qutab Buktiar Kaki of Delhi and the Guru of the celebrated saint Nizam-ud-Din Aulia. He died in A.D.1266 at Pakpattan, west Punjab and a tomb was erected in his memory. Among his Shlokas are found eighteen Shlokas of the Sikh Gurus.

3.  NAMDEV          60 hymns

Namdev was a Maharashtrian. He was born in A.D.1270 at Narsi Bamani in the district of Satara, Bombay. His father was a calico-printer named Damasheti. The name of his mother was Goona Bai, who was the daughter of a tailor of Kalyan in the same district. He was married to Raja Bai, daughter of Govind Sheti from whom he had four sons and one daughter. It is said that his devotion was so great that God came to him in physical form and freely partook of his offerings. During his lifetime Namdev visited Punjab. There is a shrine in his name at village Ghuman of Gurdaspur district. He was a Vaishnava in his early years, but became

114

a saint of the Nirguna school later on.

## 4. TRILOCHAN ·    4 hymns

Trilochan is said to have been born in A.D.1267 at Barsi in Sholapur district, Bombay. He was a Vaishya by caste. He was a contemporary of Namdev and remained in his company for some time.

## 5. PARMANAND    One hymn

Parmanand is said to have lived at Barsi in Sholapur district, Bombay. The dates of his birth and death are not known. According to the author of *Hindi Shabda Sagar*, Parmanand was a resident of Kanauj and a Brahmin by caste.

## 6. SADHNA    · One hymn

Sadhna, a butcher by trade, was a contemporary of Namdev. He is said to have been born in Sehwan in Sind.

## 7. BENI    Three hymns

Nothing is known about the life of Beni, who seems to belong to a comparatively earlier date because of the language of his hymns.

## 8. RAMANANDA    One hymn

Ramananda is said to have been born in a family of Gaur Brahmins at Mailkot, where Ramanuja had set up an idol of Vishnu, but some believe that he was the son of a Kankubaj Brahmin named Bhur Karma of Prayag. The exact date of his birth is not known. He belonged to the school of Ramanuja, but later on after pilgrimage of holy places, he brought about a reformation and started a new sect with emphasis on the devotion to Lord Rama and Sita instead of Lord Krishna and Radha. He broke down the barriers of caste and accepted several disciples from Shudras. Among the saint-poets of the *Guru Granth Sahib*, Pipa, Sain,

Dhanna, Ravidas and Kabir were his disciples. In his later years he became a saint of the Nirguna school. His discipies mentioned above also belonged to this school. He passed away at Varanasi.

## 9. DHANNA  Four hymns

Dhanna or Dhanna Jat (peasant) is said to have been born in A.D.1415. He was the resident of the village of Dhuan, a few miles away from Deoli in Rajputana. He was an idolator in the beginning, but became a monotheist later on.

## 10. PIPA  One hymn

Pipa was a king of Gagaraungarh. He was born in A.D.1425. It is said that he was a worshipper of Durga in the beginning, but he became a disciple of Ramananda later on.

## 11. SAIN  One hymn

Sain was a barber at the court of Raja Ram, the king of Rewa. He is said to have lived in the end of the fourteenth and the beginning of the fifteenth century. He was a disciple of Ramananda.

## 12. KABIR  292 hymns including Pauris of Bawan Akhri, Thittin, Var Sat and 249 Sholkas.

Kabir was born in A.D.1398 of a Brahmin virgin widow, who threw him by the side of a tank near Varanasi. From there he was picked up by a Muslim weaver named Niru and his wife Nima. He was brought up in this Muslim family. He became a disciple of Ramananda. His fame as a saint spread far and wide. He was tortured by the king Sikandar Khan Lodhi for his ideology, but he escaped all his ordeals. He founded a religious sect, which is known as Kabir Panth. His verses are found in *Bijak* and *Guru Granth Sahib*. He died at Magahar in A.D.1518. Among his Shlokas in the *Guru Granth Sahib* are found one Shloka of Namdev, one of Ravidas, one of Guru Amar Das and four of Guru Arjan Dev.

13. RAVIDAS       41 hymns

Ravidas was another disciple of Ramanada. He was a cobbler.

# THE SIKH GURUS

1. GURU NANAK DEV       974 hymns including Pauris and Shlokas.

Guru Nanak Dev, the founder of Sikhism, was born in A.D. 1469 at Talwandi (Nankana Sahib), district Sheikhupura (now in Pakistan). His father was Mehta Kalu and mother Tripta. He was married to Sulakhni, the daughter of Mula of Batala, district Gurdaspur. He had two sons namely Sri Chand and Lakhmi Das. For some time he served as in-charge of the store-house of Nawab Daulat Khan of Sultanpur after which the call of the Holy Mission came to him and he went out to preach his message of love. He visited the holy places of Hindus and Muslims both and impressed upon the leaders of both the religions to do away with all formalism and ritualism and understand the reality. In the later part of his life, he settled at Kartarpur on the banks of Ravi and passed away in A.D. 1538.

2. GURU ANGAD DEV       62 Shlokas

Guru angad Dev was born in A.D. 1504 at Sarai Matta in Ferozepore district, Punjab. His father, Pheru was a trader. Before becoming the Guru, his name was Lehna. He was married to a lady named Khiwi. He had two sons named Dasu and Datu and one daughter named Bibi Amro. At first he was a devotee of Durga, but when he came into contact with Guru Nanak Dev, he became his disciple. His service to Guru Nanak Dev was so sincere and great that Guruship was bestowed on him in A.D. 1537. He passed the rest of his life at Khadur and died there in A.D. 1553.

3. GURU AMAR DAS 907 hymns including Pauris and Shlokas

Guru Amar Das was born at Basarke in Amritsar district in

A.D.1479. He had two sons Mohan and Mori and two daughters Dani and Bhani. He was earlier a Vaishnava, but when he came into contact with Guru Angad Dev, he became his disciple. He served the Guru with such zeal and reverence that Guruship was bestowed upon him in A.D.1553. Then he went to Goindwal to live there. He passed away there in A.D.1574 at the age of 95.

| 4. | GURU RAM DAS | 679 hymns including Pauris and Shlokas. |

Guru Ram Das was born at Lahore in A.D.1534. He was married to Bibi Bhani, the daughter of Guru Amar Das. He had three sons namely Prithi chand, Mahadev and Guru Arjan Dev. Guru Amar Das installed him as Guru in A.D.1574. He began the construction of the tank at the new town named Guru Ka Chak, which was later on called Amritsar. He passed away in A.D.1581 at Goindwal.

| 5. | GURU ARJAN DEV | 2218 hymns including Pauris and Shlokas. |

Guru Arjan Dev was born in A.D.1563. He became the Guru at the age of eighteen in A.D.1581. He completed the construction of the tank and built the temple (called Golden Temple) in its midst. He was the editor and compiler of *Granth Sahib* and the majority of the verses of *Guru Granth Sahib* were composed by him. He was the first martyr of the Sikh Community. The Mughal Emperor Jehangir was responsible for his martyrdom in A.D.1606.

The sixth, seventh and eighth Sikh Gurus (Guru Har Govind, Guru Har Rai and Guru Har Krishan respectively) did not compose the bani.

| 6. | GURU TEGH BAHADUR | 59 hymns and 56 Shlokas |

Guru Tegh Bahadur was the son of the sixth Guru and was born in A.D.1622 at Amritsar. His mother was Nanaki. He was installed as a Guru in A.D.1664. In order to save the Hindus from the communal frenzy of the Mughal Emperor Aurangzeb, he attained martyrdom in A.D.1675.

7.   GURU GOBIND SINGH        One Shloka among the Shalokas of
                              Guru Tegh Bahadur said to be com-
                              posed by him.

Guru Gobind Singh, the tenth Guru, was born at Patna in A.D.1666,
when his father Guru Tegh Bahadur (the ninth Sikh Guru) was on a visit
to the holy places, while proceeding towards Assam. He became the Guru
at the age of nine. He had four sons, the two younger ones were bricked
alive at Sirhind and the elder two fought bravely in the battlefield at
Chamkaur and attained martyrdom. He wrote several longer poems of
religious and literary merit which were later compiled in the *Dasam
Granth*. He passed most of his lifetime in fighting with the opposing
forces. He gave the form of soldiers to the saintly disciples of Guru Nanak
Dev ji and named them *Khalsa*. After the death of Aurangzeb, he
accompanied his successor Bahadur Shah to Deccan, where he met Banda
Bahadur. He passed away at Nanded in A.D.1708, but before his death,
he passed on the Guruship to *Granth Sahib*. He is said to have composed
one Shloka in response to a Shloka of his father, though the authorship of
his Shloka is not mentioned in *Guru Granth Sahib*.


## THE SAINTS AND BARDS OF THE TIMES OF THE GURUS

1.   BHIKHAN  Two hymns

Bhikhan was a Sufi saint. He was a resident of Kakori in Lucknow
district of Uttar Pradesh and died in the early part of the reign of Akbar,
the Great Mughal Emperor.

2.   SUR DAS            two hymns

Sur Das, a Brahmin by caste, was born in A.D.1528. He was
appointed as Governor of the province of Sandila by the Mughal Emperor
Akbar. He is said to have squandered the revenues of the province on the
saints and fled away fearing the displeasure of the king. He was later on
arrested and imprisoned, but released shortly afterwards. He should not
be confounded with the blind Hindi Poet Sur Das, the author of *Sur Sagar*.

| 3. | SUNDAR | One Poem entitled Sad containing six Pauris. |

Sundar, who composed Sad in Ramkali Raga, depicting the death of Guru Amar Das, was one of his grandsons.

| 4. | MARDANA | Three Shlokas |

Mardana was the bard who accompanied Guru Nanak Dev during his travels.

| 5. | KAL | 49 (46 Swayyas and 3 Sorathas) |
| 6. | KALSAHAR | 4 Swayyas |
| 7. | TAL | 1 Swayya |
| 8. | JALAP | 4 Swayyas |
| 9. | JAL | 1 Swayya |
| 10. | KIRAT | 8 Swayyas |
| 11. | SAL | 3 Swayyas |
| 12. | BHAL | 1 Swayya |
| 13. | NAL | 6 Swayyas |
| 14. | BHIKHA | 2 Swayyas |
| 15. | JALAN | 1 Swayya |
| 16. | DAS | 14 (7 Swayyas, 3 Rad and 4 Jholnay) |
| 17. | GAYAND | 5 Swayyas |
| 18. | SEWAK | 7 Swayyas |
| 19. | MATHURA | 10 Swayyas |
| 20. | BAL | 5 Swayyas |
| 21. | HARBANS | 2 Swayyas |
| 22 & | | |
| 23. | SATTA AND BALWAND | One Var containing eight Pauris. |

Satta and Balwand were the bards in the court of Guru Arjan Dev. They sang a Var in Ramkali Raga in the praise of the first five Gurus.

Some scholars are of the view that the bards mentioned from No.5 to No.21 were actually not seventeen. They were only eleven. According to them Kal and Kalsahar are the same. Similarly Jalap and Jal are one and the same. Das and Sewak are not the names of the bards. Through these names, the poets have exhibited their humility. According to them, the word "Gang" occurring in the Swayyas may not be taken as the name of a bard. Tal and Gayand are also not the names of the bards. Some of the bards came in the court of Guru Amar Das, some in the court of Guru Ram Das and the remaining in the court of Guru Arjan Dev.

## REFERENCE

1.  Equipped for Every Good Work published in 1946 by Watchtower Bible and Tract Society, Inc. International Bible Students Association, Brooklyn, New York, U.S.A. P.10.

# V

# Religious Philosophy of Guru Granth Sahib

## MEANS OF KNOWLEDGE:

The Sikh Philosophy recognises three means of knowledge viz. perception, inference and scriptural testimony. The perception includes the perception of ordinary persons i.e. the contact of the soul with the sense-organs and objects through mind, the perception of the 'liberated souls' e.g. the Guru and the True Sikh and the Perception of God Himself. The world, according to Sikhism, is not a mere appearance, it is definitely real. Even, with the attainment of final beatitude, the world remains real. The Guru and the True Sikh perceive everywhere the grandeur of Brahman. God Perceives His Creation and Enjoys the Sport (lila). The second source of knowledge i.e. inference is based on perceptual knowledge. It includes comparison and presumption as well. The third source of knowledge is Shabda or verbal testimony. The testimony may either be sacred or secular. Adopting the above-mentioned three sources of knowledge, the religious philosophy of the *Guru Granth Sahib* presents forth the following thoughts about *Brahman, Jiva* and *Maya*.

## BRAHMAN (GOD):

Brahman is One without a second. His Name is Truth. He is the Creator. He is without Fear and Enmity. He is Immortal, Unborn and Self-Existent. He is Truth, Consciousness and Bliss. He is Omnipresent, Omnipotent and Omniscient. He is Changeless and Flawless. When He Wills, He becomes Many. He begins His Sport like a Juggler. He Creates the universe and brings the matter out of Himself. Before the creation, He is in abstract meditation (*Sunn-Samadhi*) and devoid of Attributes (*Nirguna*) but after the creation, He, as Ishvara, manifests Himself as

122

treasure-house of qualities *(Saguna)*. He is Faultless, Good, Holy, Light, Primal-Cause and Essence, Beyond our congnizance, Pervasive and Everlasting. He does not Incarnate. All the gods and goddesses are His Creation. He is a *Purusha*, Who Creates the whole universe. There is none other separate Eternal Entity except Brahman. He is the Creator of the Prakriti of three *gunas* (qualities) i.e. *rajas* (activity), *tamas* (morbidity) and *sattva* (rhythm), He is a *Purusha*, distinct from other *Purushas* (Jivas/ souls). He is *Adi Purakh* (Who is from the very beginning), *Sat Purakh* (Pervasive and Overlasting), *Karta Purakh* (Creator), *Akal Purakh* (Uninfluenced by Time) and *Niranjan Purakh* (without the influence of Maya).

## JIVA:

Jiva is a part and parcel of Brahman. It should not be mistaken for Brahman Himself. It has its own individuality, but since it is a part of Brahman, it carries the qualities of Brahman. It is immortal like Brahman, but works under the Will of Brahman. The physical body decays, but it continues for ever.

## MAYA:

According to *Guru Granth Sahib*, *Prakriti* or *Maya* is not a separate Ultimate Reality. It has been created by God. It takes the individual away from God and thus leads him towards transmigration. When the influence of maya vanishes, the Jiva realises Brahman. When Brahman comes into contact with maya of three *gunas* (qualities), the process of creation begins. The unconscious matter and the finite selves, which exist in Brahman before the creation, join this process by a Gracious Act of His Will. Maya is the bondage for Jiva and its main functionary is ego. The three *gunas* are the resultant of ego or *Ahamkara*.

Other aspects of the religious philosophy of sikhism are given hereunder:

## CREATION:

The Sikh Gurus are of the view that it is wrong to delimit the

Creation of the Lord. Whereas the Lord Himself is without limits, His creation cannot be considered within limits. There are countless universes and in them there are many species of diverse forms and colours. The Pauranic idea of eighty-four lakhs of species is found in Guru Granth Sahib. There are lakhs and crores of upper and nether regions. Guru Nanak Dev says, "From God arose air, from air water, from water the three worlds, with His Light in every self." The theory of creation expounded by the Sikh Gurus resembles *Brahmparinamavada* of Ramanuja, which presents forth the Samkhyan theory of evolution, but emphasises that Prakriti is absolutely dependent upon God. Guru Nanak Dev says, "Nobody knows the exact time, when the universe was created except the Creator Himself."

## MICROCOSM:

The Truth (Brahman) is Immanent in the universe. The human body is its repository. The body is not merely a thing like other objects. It is an epitome of the universe. It is a microcosm, whereas the universe is macrocosm. Therefore whatever exists in the universe, also exists in the body of the human being. This implies that the same energy is in action, both in the human body and the vast cosmos, therefore the seeker should not get himseelf lost in the vastness of the cosmos and only concentrate himself on the Truth within his own body.

## KARMA:

Every Jiva desires, thinks and acts. Every action has its association in the past, present and future. Every action is like a seed sown in the body, which is a field of action. When the seed of action is sown, the consequences must follow. A Jiva repeatedly experiences births nd deaths because of his action in this world. This is the theory of Karma or the moral law of causation. There are two types of Karmas i.e. the higher Karmas and the lower karmas. The works ordained by Shastric injunctions are considered lower Karmas in *Guru Granth Sahib*, therefore they are rejected. The emphasis has been laid on the higher Karmas, which lead on to the realisation of Brahman. The worldly Karmas may be good or bad, virtuous or sinful. The remuneration of these Karmas depends on

124

their quality. Whatever one did in his previous births, that makes his present life. It is futile to slander others for the actions done. the fault lies in one's own actions. The karmas done under the influence of maya and ego are the cause of transmigration. The soul takes various physical forms according to its karmas. It experiences bondage, when it enters the field of action. Every action enchains him further. It tightens the noose around his neck. Transmigration ceases with the exhaustion of desire, but the desire (Trishna) comes to an end only, when we meet the True Guru, who is the Knower of Brahman and act according to his instructions. The Guru gives to the disciple the Name of the Lord, which is the panacea of all ills.

## GRACE:

Though we get our body on account of our karmas, the release can only be obtained through the Grace of the Lord. The Grace of the Lord begins with our acceptance of the True Path in life. All the creation works under the *Hukam* or the Laws of God. These Laws are true for all times and work in all the three fields i.e. physical, moral, and spiritual. All the creatures in the world are bound by these Laws. The Law of cause and effect works in every field. The amount of the Grace of the Lord necessitates our accomplishments on the right Path. In fact, the Grace of the Lord is not the result of any whim of the Lord, it begins and matures with the beginning and maturity of our *Dharma*.

## VIRTUE AND VICE:

In Sikhism, the performance of duty i.e. *Dharma*, does not mean the observance of the formal ritualism on the pursuance of the Shastric injunctions. The Sikh Gurus laid down definite moral code, which enjoins a Sikh to do such actions which are called higher karmas. The practice of these higher karmas is the practice of virtues in life. The Sikh has to imbibe the godly qualities in his life. These qualities include Truth, Purity, Justice, Sweetness, Fearlessness, Mercy etc. The five major vices can be overcome with the practice of five virtues i.e. the lust can be overcome with self-control, anger with toleration, greed with contentment, worldly affection with devotion to duty and ego with modesty. The virtue and vice are both the Creation of God. Vice is a sin. It is impure and

125

unclean. God is Pure. An individual becomes godlike to the extent he becomes pure. In a world vitiated by all types of ills, one should avoid indulgence to the extreme and also avoid self-mortification. On both the sides, one loses balance, therefore the middle path is to be followed, which is the golden mean. One has neither to renounce the world or jump in the field of action like an unbridled horse. The foremost duty of an individual is to understand *Dharma* or the path of piety. The piety can be achieved by the control of our senses. The five senses of sight, hearing, taste, smell and touch are to be kept under discipline.

## EGO:

The path of ego is averse to the path of devotion. Modesty is a prerequisite to the path of devotion. The path of ego is the path of destruction. Whosoever thinks high of himself, is reduced to dust in a moment. Ego is the principle and subtle vice. It is always present in a Jiva in one form or the other. It is the I-ness which spoils the fruit of great penances. The Truth or the Fourth State is never realised in ego. The Fourth State or the Supreme State *(Param Pad)* is an egoless state.

## MIND AND INTELLECT:

The mind and intellect are the outer coverings of the soul undergoing transmigration. The light of mind is eclipsed by the dirt of ego, which has blackened it in the course of several births. The mind is puffed up with ego, but in its original form, the mind is identical with *Jivatma* (soul). In order to control the mind, its reins should be tightened. It is not an easy job to bring the mind under control. The great sages have failed in their attempts. When the disciple follows the discipline ordained by the Guru, he comes to know the nature of mind. He realises that the mind is like an intoxicated elephant and only the goad of the Guru can give it a new life. The Grace of the Lord and Guru play a great part in the conquest of mind. When the mind is conquered, the Lord is realised and the whole world is conquered. The intellect makes one wise and educated. The education makes us realise the Truth. The Gurus are in favour of *Para Vidya* or the spiritual education. For them the verbal testimony is the vital source of knowledge. The *Granth (Pothi)* is the Abode of the Lord. The education

126

creates such intellect as helps us to subdue the mind and realise the Lord.

## DEATH:

Death is a reality. Whosoever is born, must die. Every moment that passes reduces the span of our life. The Jiva does not realise it. The soul is eternal. The death lays its hand only on the body, but nothing is destroyed. The air mixes with air, light in light, earth in earth. When the gross body dies, the subtle body of the soul consisting of vital breath (Prana), mind and intellect lives. This subtle body also dies, when the state of final emancipation is realised. When, after death, the soul appears before Dharmaraja (the god of Justice), a decision is taken about its future according to its actions in the material world. It may be sent to be reborn as an animal, a bird or an insect. It may even be sent to the higher planes of gods or it may be sent to be born again as a human being for its further development.

## HEALTH:

The Sikh Religion recognises the human body as the abode of God. It is the temple of God, wherein the individual can see His Light. A healthy mind lives in a healthy body. The gods are said to have a burning desire for the human body, which is the only medium, through which the soul reaches the desired goal. Like other temples, the temple of human body has to be kept neat and clean with full veneration. It should be made a befitting house for the Lord. The cleanliness of mind and body takes the individual soul nearer God. The Gurus have laid emphasis on continence (Sanyam). Over-eating or gluttony is bad. Under-nourishment is still worse. A balanced diet is necessary for the upkeep of health. A hungry person cannot be a healthy constituent of society. He cannot even think of God. Such foods only should be eaten, which do not upset the physical and mental balance. Therefore the use of intoxicants has been strictly forbidden, which destroy our happiness, create pains in the body and bring up vices in the mind. For the upkeep of health, it is necessary to rise early in the morning. The Sikh of the Guru should eat less and sleep less.

127

## YOGA:

The beliefs and practices of contemporary Yogis were not liked by Guru Nanak Dev. He rejected outright all their formalism. He said, "Yoga does not consist in wearing patched quilt, in carrying staff and smearing the body with ashes. Yoga does not consist in wearing ear-rings, in cutting hair and playing on *Singhi* (a musical instrument). Yoga does not consist in going to the cremation ground and roaming about in the country. . . ." According to the Guru, the true Yoga consists in the meditation on the Word and the repetition of the Name of the Lord. The Yogi remains unaffected by maya, just as the lotus remains above the surface of water. The Yoga of the Sikh Gurus is a balanced union of action, devotion and knowledge.

## BHAKTI:

The real devotion of the Lord is His Love. There are two types of devotion (*Bhakti*) i.e. *Antarang* (inward) and *Behrang* (outward). *Guru Granth Sahib* rejects the outward or formalistic devotion. It lays emphasis on the inward devotion of pure love. *Bhakti* is the real path towards *Nirvana*. The final emancipation can never be attained through learning and guises. The world is mad without Bhakti. Without Bhakti, the human being appears as a dog or a swine. The Bhakta (devotee) is full of undefiled fear and pure love; fear of the Omnipotent and love of the Merciful and Compassionate Lord. The Word of the Guru is the treasure-house of devotion. Whosoever sings, listens or practises it, attains his objective. The Name of the Lord is instilled in his being and the union of the soul and the Higher Soul is achieved.

## GURU AND NAME:

In every walk of life, one needs a guide. Similar is the case in spiritual domain. For our spiritual uplift, we need a Guru or religious preceptor, who prepares us in thought, deed and action in order to make us a loving bride of the Lord. The Guru or Satguru is the kindly light, which sheds lustre on our path. The ten Gurus of the Sikhs are the ten manifestations of the Guru-soul. The last Sikh Guru, Guru Gobind Singh, bestowed the status of the Guru on *Granth Sahib* (the *Adi Granth*). The Guru-Soul manifested itself in the form of *WORD, NAME* or *BANI*. The *Word* or the *mantra* of the Guru is the Guru himself, therefore the greatest service of the Guru consists in the repetition of the mantra with faith and love. None of the meritorious works equals the Name of the Lord. All the sins are washed away with it. The name and ego cannot live at one plane. The Name saves the Jiva from the dreadful *Yama*. The true devotee remembers the Lord in all his actions and postures i.e. standing, sleeping or waking.

## HOLY CONGREGATION:

The holy congregation *(Sadh Sangat or Satsang)* of the Sikhs meets in a temple *(Gurdwara)*, where it recites the Name of the Lord and sings the *bani* (compositions) of the Guru from *Guru Granth Sahib*. This congregation is like a philosopher's stone, which turns ordinary people into gold. The member of this congregation is in love with the Name of the Lord and ultimately realises TRUTH (The Lord). This congregation is like a boat, which takes the inmate beyond the world-ocean, where there is no birth and death. The pure intellect dawns upon him and his overturned mind-lotus blossoms. He is cool, calm and content. All his desires are extinguished. The mind does not run in diverse directions and the Pure Abode of the Lord is achieved. The holy congregation is a school of the True Guru, where the devotee learns about the qualities of the Lord, which he has to imbibe within himself. The main function of *Sadh Sangat* is the remembrance of the Name of the Lord. For this purpose each disciple concentrates on the WORD and the music of the sweet songs of the Guru not only helps him to drink deep the nectar of *bani*, but also helps him further in spiritual flights. Singing of *Gur-bani* is known as *Kirtan*. Whosoever listens to or sings the *Kirtan* of Hari, no trouble can come near him. *Kirtan* is the food of divine love.

## A TRUE SIKH:

*Guru Granth Sahib* decries any distinction of caste. No devotee considers himself superior to any other. Humility and modesty are his specialties, therefore the service of humanity is the main aim of his life.

He is a saint, soldier and scholar, therefore the society of which he is the constituent is martial in spirit, saintly in character and scholarly in knowledge. The religion of the *Guru Granth Sahib* is the religion of activity. It enjoins every devotee to lead the life of a householder. It rejects *varnas* (castes) and *ashramas* (stages of life) and lay emphasis on equality and fraternity. The adherent of the discipline enunciated in *Guru Granth Sahib* has to work and earn for himself and his family and is even in a position to give tithe *(daswadh)* for the good of others Whereas, following the path of *Dharma*, he realises *Moksha* (final emancipation), he also makes appropriate use of *Artha* (material gains) and *Kama* (worldly desires).

AN IDEAL SOCIETY:

According to the *Guru Granth Sahib*, the responsibility of the society rests on the shoulders of the State. The king or the Chief of the State should be an ideal personality in whom all his subjects can repose confidence. He should be the humble servant of the poor. He should follow the democratic principles, without which his kingdom is sure to fall after some time. Woman is the most significant part of the society; she gives birth to the greatest individuals of society. She should receive the utmost reverence. She has an equal right to grow spiritually, equal right to attend religious congregations and recite divine hymns in the temples. As a daughter, sister, mother and wife, she should receive due respect.

CEREMONIES:

The Sikh Gurus have rejected the performance of all kinds of works, which result in ego and duality. For them all those actions are commendable which help us in the realisation of our ultimate objective i.e. the Union with the Lord. Guru Arjan Dev says, "All other works are useless except those about the Lord." There are no rituals and formal ceremonies which must be performed by the adherent of *Guru Granth Sahib*. A Sikh is a saint and a saint has nothing else to do except to adore his Guru and follow his instructions. His primary function is the remembrance of the Name of the Lord. His Guru is *Guru Granth Sahib*, for whose instructions, he has to meet the holy congregation in the Gurdwara. He is also a householder. The male has to earn the bread for the family and the female has to look after the upkeep of the house and the welfare of the family. Thus a Sikh has to perform twin duties, the secular as well as divine. His secular duties also verge on the divine border, because in every work, he has to seek the divine Grace. According to Guru Ram Das, whosoever calls himself a Sikh of the True Guru, gets up in the early hours of the morning and remembers the Name of the Lord. He takes a bath in the tank of nectar and under the instructions of the Guru recites the Name of Hari. In this way, he sheds off all his sins. He sings the *bani* of the Guru and remembers the Name of the Lord, while sitting and standing. He works with his hands and feet and in his heart, he is attuned with the Lord.

GOD-REALISATION:

Guru Granth Sahib considers Gon-realisation as the chief objective of human life. The human body is the only medium, through which the objective can be fulfilled. The qualities or virtues form the foundation on which the spiritual edifice can be raised. With these qualities, the self shines like a mirror, in which the Higher Soul Manifests Itself. The selfless action, devotion and knowledge put us on the right pathway, because the Grace of the Lord begins at the very outset and the resultant is God-realisation. The Guru gives us knowledge; the Word given by him creates devotion and selfless action. By the Grace of the Lord, we meet the Guru and by the Grace of the Guru, we meet the Lord. The State of God-realisation is known as *Sahaj*. It is also known as *Chautha Pad* (the Fourth State) and *Param Pad* or the Supreme State. It is called the Fourth State because it is beyond the other three states of awakening *(Jagrit)*, dream *(Svapan)* and dreamless sleep *(Sushupti)*. It is also beyond the three qualities of *Rajas, Tamas* and *Sattva*, which are the constituents of *Maya*. There are some obstacles in the way of God-realisation and the remembrance of the Name of the Lord. These obstacles are idleness, worldly thoughts, sleep and the power to perform miracles. The Guru has cautioned the disciples about these ills. The Union of the soul and the Higher Soul is known as Yoga in India philosophy. The Yoga of the Guru Granth Sahib is called *Sahaj Yoga, Name Yogha* or *Surt-Shabad Yoga*. The concept of *Nirvana* in Sikhism is different from that of other Indian

131

religions. The Sikh has no desire to enter heaven. He even discards *Mukti* as defined in *Shastras*. He wants to remain always at the Feet of the Lord, filled with extreme devotion and love. God-realisation is the result of both effort and Grace. Guru Nanak Dev has mentioned five regions *(khands)* in the process of God-realization. The first region is the region of *Dharma* (piety) and the fifth and the last is that of Truth. The maturity of pious actions leads the seeker to the second region called the region of knowledge *(Gyan)*. In this region, he becomes aware of the vastness of the universe i.e. the infinite expanse of the creation. With the maturity of knowledge, the seeker enters the third region of Effort *(Saram)*. In this region of beauty, his mind and intellect become superfine. This brings the seeker to the fourth region of Grace *(Karam)*, where he attains the necessary spiritual strength to enter the fifth and the last region of TRUTH *(Sach)*. In this region, the journey of the seeker comes to an end. He realises Truth i.e. GOD.

# Bibliography

*Adi Granth*, The, Munshi Ram Manohar Lal, New Delhi, 1970.

*Adi Sri Guru Granth Sahib*, S.G.P.C., Amritsar, 1978.

Ahluwalia, Jasbir Singh, *Metaphysical Problems of Sikhism*, Godwin Publishers, Chandigarh, 1976.

Ahuja, N.D., *Great Guru Nanak and Muslims*, Kirti Publishing House, Chandigarh.

Ajit Singh & Rajinder Singh (eds) *Glimpses of Sikh Religion*, National Book Shop, Delhi, 1987.

————, *Studies in Guru Nanak, 3 Vols.*, National Book Shop, - Delhi, 1987.

Anand, Balwant Singh, *Guru Nanak: Religion and Ethics*, Punjabi University, Patiala, 1968.

Avtar Singh, *Ethics of the Sikhs*, Punjabi University, Patiala.

Benerjee, Anil Chandra, *Guru Nanak and His Times*, Punjabi University, Patiala.a

———— *Guru Nanak to Gobind Singh*, Rajesh Publishers, Allahabad, 1978.

Banerjee, Indu Bhushan, *Evolution of the Khalsa*, Calcutta, 1946

Barrier, N.G., *The Sikhs and Their Literature*, New Delhi, 1970.

Bhave, Vinoba, *Comments on Japuji, Guru Nanak's Great Composition*, Punjabi University, Patiala, 1973.

Caveshar, Sardul Singh, *Sikh Studies*, 1939.

Chawala, Harbans Singh (ed), *Guru Nanak: The Prophet of the people*, Gurdwara Sri Guru Singh Sabha, New Delhi, 1970

Cole, W. Owen, *Sikhism and its Indian Content (1469-1708)*, D.K. Agencies (P) Ltd., New Delhi, 1984.

————, *Guru in Sikhism*

Cole, W. Owen and Sambhi, Piara Singh, *The Sikhs, Their Religion, Beliefs and Practices*, Vikas Publishing House, New Delhi, 1980.

Dalip Singh, *Sikhism: A Modern and Psychological Perspective*, Bahri Publications, New Delhi, 1979.

————, *Universal Sikhism: An Aid to Moral Upliftment*, Bahri Publications, New Delhi, 1979.

————, *Yoga and Sikh Teachings, Some Questions*, Bahri Publications,

133

New Delhi, 1979.

Daljeet Singh, *Sikhism: A Comparative Study of its Theology and Mysticism,* Sterling Publishers, New Delhi, 1979.

———, *The Sikh Ideology,* Guru Nanak Foundation, New Delhi.

Darshan Singh, *Indian Bhakti Tradition, and Sikh Gurus,* Punjab Publishers, Chandigarh, 1968.

———, *Relgion of Guru Nanak,* Lyall Book Depot, Ludhiana, 1970.

Deol, Gurdev Singh, *Socal & Political Philosophy of Guru Nanak Dev, and Guru Gobind Singh,* New Academic Publishing Co, Jullunder, 1976.

Dhillon, Dalbir Singh (Dr.), *Sikhism, Origin and Development,* Atlantic Publishers and Distributors, New Delhi, 1988.

Dorothy Field, *Religion of the Sikhs,* Ess Ess Publications, Delhi, 1976.

Duggal, Kartar Singh, *Sikh Gurus; Their Life and Tteachings,* Vikas Publishing House, New Delhi, 1980.

Francis, Eric, *Guru Nanak,* Purohit and Sons, Bombay, 1970.

Ganda Singh, *The Sikhs and Sikhism,* Sikh History Society, Patiala, 1959.

———, *The Sikhs and their Religion,* The Sikh Foundation, California, 1974.

———, (ed) *Source Book on Guru Nanak's Life and Teachings,* Punjabi University, Patiala, 1969.

Ganda Singh (Gyani), *Lives of Sikh Gurus, and Basic Principles of Sikh Gurus,* Khalsa Diwan, Malaya, Ipoh, Malayisa, 1962.

Gill, Pritam Singh, *Concept of Sikhism,* New Academic Publishing Co., Jullunder, 1979.

———, *Trinity of Sikhism, Philosophy, Religion and State,* New Academic Publishing Co., Jullunder, 1973.

Gopal Singh, *Religion of the Sikhs,* Asia Publishing House, Bombay, 1972.

———, *The Sikh, Their History, Religion & Culture, Ceremonies and Literature,* Popular Parkashan, Bombay, 1970.

———, *Sri Guru Granth Sahib,* Gurdas Kapur & Sons, (P) Ltd., Delhi, 1960.

———, *Guru Nanak's Relevance to our times,* Guru Nanak Foundation, New Delhi.

Greenles, Duncan, *The Gospel of the Guru Granth Sahib,* Theosophical, Publishing House, Madras, 1975.

Gupta, B.S., *Rock and the Pool: Guru Nanak Themes,* National Book Organisation, Delhi, 1968.

Gurdev Singh (ed), *Perspectives on Sikh Tradition,* Siddharta Publications, Chandigarh, 1986.

Gurmit Singh, *A Critique of Sikhism,* Faqir Singh & Sons, Amritsar. 1969.

Gurnam Kaur, *Reason and Revelation in Sikhism.*

Harbans Singh, *Faith of the Sikhs,* Guru Nanak Foundation, New Delhi.

————, *The Message of Sikhism,* Gurdwara Parbandhak Committee, Delhi, 1968.

Harbans Singh (Dr.) *Degh, Tegh, Fateh,* Alam Publishing House, Chandigarh, 1968.

Harnam Singh, *Sikh Religion, Karma and Transmigration,* the author, Jullunder, 1955.

Hochline, C.H., *The Sikh & their Scriptures*

Isher Singh, *Nanakism, A New World Order, Temporal and Spiritual,* Ranjit Publishing House, New Delhi, 1976.

————, *Philosophy of Guru Nanak - A Comparative Study,* Ranjit Publishing House, Delhi, 1969.

Jagjit Singh, *The Sikh Religion; A Perspective Study,* Bahri Publications, New Delhi, 1981.

Jain, S.C., *A Panorama of Sikh Relgion and Philosophy,* Bahabali Publications, New Delhi, 1985.

Jodh Singh, Dr., *Religious Philosophy of Guru Nanak,* National Book Shop, Delhi, 1989.

Johar, Surinder Singh, *Handbook on Sikhs,* Vivek, Delhi, 1977.

Kapur, B.L., *Message of Shri Guru Nanak Dev in the context of Sanatanist Tradition,* Qaumi Press, Jullunder, 1967.

Khazan Singh, *History and Philosophy of the Sikhs,* 2 Vols.

Khushwant Singh, *Religion of Sikhs,* University of Madras, Madras, 1969.

Kohli, S.S., *Philosophy of Guru Nanak,* Punjab University, Chandigarh, 1969.

————, *Outlines of Sikh Thought,* Punjabi Parkashak, Delhi, 1966.

————, *Sikh Ethics,* Munshiram Manohar Lal, Delhi, 1973.

————, *A Critical Study of the Adi-Granth,* The Punjabi Writers Co-Operative Society, Ltd., New Delhi, 1961.

Lajwanti Lahori, *The Concept of Man in Sikhism,* Munshiram Manohar Lal, Publishers (P) Ltd., Delhi, 1985.

Macauliffe, Max Arthur, *The Sikh Religion,* 6 Vols, S.Chand & Co., Delhi, 1963.

Manmohan Singh, *Guru Granth Sahib,* 8 Vols., S.G.P.C., Amritsar, 1981.

Mansukhani, Dr. Gobind Singh, *A Book of Sikh Studies,* National Book Shop, Delhi, 1989.

135

————, *Aspects of Sikhism*, Punjabi Writers Co-operative, Industrial Society Ltd., New Delhi.

————, *The Quintessence of Sikhism*, S.G.P.C., Amritsar, 1986.

————. *Introduction to Sikhism*, Hemkunt Press, New Delhi, 1989.

Mcleod, W.H., *Early Sikh Tradition: A study of the Janam-Sakhis*, Clarendon Press, Oxford, 1980.

————, *Guru Nanak and the Sikh Religion*, Oxford University Press, Bombay, 1969.

Mrigendra Singh, *Miraculous Guru Nanak*, Robert Spedler & Sons, New York, 1977.

Narang, Gokul Chand, *Glorious History of Sikhism*, New Book Society of India, New Delhi, 1972.

————, *Transformation of Sikhism.*

Nirbhai Singh, *Philosophy of Sikhism*, Atlantic Publishers & Distributors, New Delhi, 1972.

Oberoi, Mohan Singh, *Sikh Mysticism: The Sevenfold Yoga of Sikhism*, the Author, Amritsar, 1964.

Raghavacar, S.S. & Rmakrishanarao, K.B. (eds), *Guru Nanak, His Life and Teachings*, Mysore University, Mysore, 1971.

Raj, Hormise Nirmal, *Evolution of the Sikh Faith*, Unity Book Service, New Delhi, 1987.

Ranbir Singh, *Glimpses of the Divine Masters*, International Traders Corporation, New Delhi, 1965.

————, *The Sikh Way of Life*, India Publishers, New Delhi, 1968.

Raj, Niharranjan, *The Sikh Gurus and the Sikh Society*, Munshiram Manohar Lal, New Delhi, 1975.

Rup Singh, *Sikhism, A Universal Relgion.*

*Sacred Writings of the Sikhs*, By Khushwant Singh, et al, George Allen, London.

Santokh Singh, *Philosophical Foundation of the Sikh Value System*, Munshiram Manohar Lal Publishers, Delhi, 1982.

Sethi, Amarjit Singh, *Universal Sikhism*, Hemkunt Press, New Delhi, 1972.

Shan, Harnam Singh, *God as Known to Guru Nanak*, Guru Nanak Viadya Bhandar Trust, Delhi, 1971.

————, *Guru Nanak's Moral Code: As Reflected in His Hymns*, Guru Nanak Foundation, Chandigarh, 1970.

Sharma, C.D., *A Critical Study of Indian Philosophy*, Moti Lal Banarasi Das, Delhi, 1973.

Sharma, Harbans Lal, *Concept of Jiva of Guru Nanak, against the*

*Background of different Indian Schools of Philosophy and Religion*, Punjabi University, Patiala, 1971.

Sher Singh, *Philosophy of Sikhism*, Sterling Publishers, Delhi, 1966.

————, (Tr., comp.) *Guru Nanak on the Malady of Man*, Sterling Publishers, New Delhi, 1968.

Sher Singh, 'Sher', *Glimpses of Sikhism and Sikhs*, Metropolitan Book Co. (P) Ltd., New Delhi, 1982.

Sikka, Ajit Singh, *Facets of Guru Nanak's Thoughts*, Bee Kay, Ludhiana, 1972.

Sobti, Harcharan Singh, *Studies in Budhism & Sikhism*, Eastern Book Linkers, Delhi, 1986.

*Studies in Sikhism and Comparative Religion*, Guru Nanak Foundation, New Delhi.

Taran Singh, *The Ideal Man of the Guru Granth*, Punjabi University, Patiala, 1966.

————, (ed) *Guru Nanak and Indian Religious Thought*, Punjabi University, Patiala, 1970.

Teja Singh, *Sikh Religion: An Outline of its Doctrines*, S.G.P.C., Amritsar, 1958.

————, *Sikhism, its ideals and institutions*, 1938.

Thompson, M.R., *Sikh Belief and Practice*, Edward Arnold, London, 1985.

Trilochan Singh, *Ethical Philosophy of Guru Nanak*, University of Calcutta, 1973.

————, *True Humanism of Guru Nanak*, S.G.P.C., Delhi, 1968.

————, *Guru Nanak's Religion*, Raj Kamal Parkshan, Delhi, 1969.

Trump, E., *The Adi Granth*, Munshi Ram Manoharlal, Delhi, 1970.

Wazir Singh, *Aspects of Guru Nanak's Philosophy*, Lahore Book Shop, Ludhiana, 1969.

————, *Guru Nanak's Theory of Truth*, Punjabi University, Patiala, 1966.

————, *Humanism of Guru Nanak: A Philosophic Enquiry*, Ess Ess Publishers, Delhi, 1977.

# Index